ALASKA BEER

ALASKA BEER

LIQUID GOLD IN THE LAND OF THE MIDNIGHT SUN

BILL HOWELL

Foreword by Geoff & Marcy Larson

AMERICAN PALATE

Published by American Palate
A Division of The History Press
Charleston, SC 29403
www.historypress.net

Cover images courtesy Elaine Howell Photography and Design.

First published 2015

Manufactured in the United States

ISBN 978.1.62619.449.6

Library of Congress Control Number: 2015931728

Notice: The information in this book is true and complete to the best of our knowledge. It is offered without guarantee on the part of the author or The History Press. The author and The History Press disclaim all liability in connection with the use of this book.

For Elaine

Contents

FOREWORD

When we first entertained the idea of brewing beer in Alaska, we had the good fortune to live in the same city that houses the Alaska State Historical Collections. While there were no breweries operating in Alaska during the mid-1980s at the time we were thinking about ours, we knew there had been many breweries in Alaska before us. We wanted to learn about what they went through and what we could expect. We found a wealth of information in those historical collections at the Alaska State Library, much of it on microfilm and tapes. It was a delight but extremely tedious to work through. We certainly wish we could have had this wonderful book by Bill Howell as a resource at that time. He has teased out of those collections an informative and entertaining tale of the state's brewing history. We knew it was there, but we certainly did not have the patience to put it all together like he did!

Our first foray into the history of beer making in Alaska unearthed an 1887 advertisement: "Pure beer made and on sale at wholesale, expressly and exclusively for Medicinal, Mechanical and scientific purposes." Say what?! Yes, the Alaska Territorial Customs Act prohibited the sale, importation and use of distilled spirits…unless it had medicinal, mechanical or scientific purposes. Seems like there was a lot of call for those purposes, and you read historical newspaper articles a little differently when you realize that. An April 9, 1887 issue of the *Alaskan* stated: "Mr. A. Cohen is having a new boiler placed in his medicinal, mechanical and scientific manufacturing establishment." Who knew a brewery could have such lofty purpose? In fact, the commissioner of Internal Revenue collected a special tax from 147 retail liquor dealers, 6 breweries, 8 retail dealers and 1 wholesale dealer in malt liquors before the start of the Klondike gold rush. It had to have been a fun time! And that was just one sliver of our storied history.

Bill Howell takes us on a journey from the beginning of our brewing roots in the far north to the present day. In Alaska, our history is a bit condensed since we are such a new territory, but it does not prevent our brewers from being just as colorful and industrious as those in the old land. Challenging the nearly impossible logistics, wildly careening "boom and bust" economics and at times strangling legal rules, the early brewers of Alaska paved the way for those of us here today. We applaud them for their perseverance, and we thank Bill for his patience and painstaking research to illuminate this rich history of brewing in Alaska. He has done us all a great service. Cheers to Bill!

—GEOFF AND MARCY LARSON
Alaskan Brewing Company

PREFACE

As a young man growing up in New Orleans, my exposure to the joys of beer drinking came early and often. The Big Easy has always had a more civilized attitude toward alcohol than most of the rest of the United States, and both my parents, being social drinkers themselves, shared the city's relaxed and tolerant attitude. With an official drinking age of only eighteen, New Orleans in the late 1970s and early '80s was a wonderful town in which to acquire knowledge about and experience with alcohol in general and beer in particular.

None of the above is to imply that New Orleans at that time was any sort of craft beer oasis—far from it. During my preteen years, there were still a few regional brewers in operation, like the Jackson Brewery, or Jax, as it was universally known in the city, but by the time I started college in 1980, only the stalwart Dixie Brewing Company, founded in 1907, was still brewing. In truth, the demise of these regionals made little difference, as all of them had been churning out the same bland light lagers as the huge national brewers. Like many of my generation, I spent my college years looking on beer as cheap, cold alcoholic refreshment; when I could afford it, I drank cocktails, not beer.

My attitude toward beer first began to change in the spring of 1984, on a trip to San Francisco, where I encountered Anchor Steam on draft. Like so many craft beer lovers of my generation, this was the beer that first opened my eyes to the true potential of beer as a beverage. I would be exaggerating if I said that it turned me into a craft beer aficionado with the first taste;

another five years would pass before I fully grasped what beer could be. But it was a start.

I graduated college in 1984, was commissioned an ensign in the U.S. Navy and spent the next five years of my life training for and then serving on my first submarine, the USS *Silversides* (SSN 679). My duty stations took me from Florida to New England to Puget Sound and finally to Virginia, but besides grabbing an Anchor Steam whenever I could find one, my next exposure to truly good beer was during port calls in Britain. Cask ale made a strong and favorable impression on me, but I assumed it was something uniquely British. It still seemed to me that it would have been too much to expect flavor like that from American beers.

My real epiphany on the subject of craft beer took place in early 1989 at a beer dinner held at a restaurant in Virginia Beach hosted by a fellow naval officer named Lyle Brown. While I parted ways with the young lady who was my date that night soon afterward, Lyle and I remain friends to this day and my love affair with craft beer that began at that dinner has only grown more intense as the decades have passed. I've forgotten the names of most of the beers I tasted that evening, but I've never forgotten how much enjoyment I got from them. Before long I had joined the local homebrew club, was brewing my own beers and had begun seeking out the best brews I could find across the United States and around the world. Traveling the world on Uncle Sam's dime made for some wonderful beer adventures, especially the three years I spent living in downtown London and hunting for great beers across Britain and much of Western Europe.

The focus of my beer interests changed when I retired from the navy in 2004 and moved to Alaska's Kenai Peninsula. Previously, where I lived was always a temporary arrangement, two or three years at most until the next set of orders sent me somewhere else. Now, Alaska would be my home for the foreseeable future, and I began to take a keen interest in not only the current state of its craft breweries but also in their past and likely future. I quickly learned that Alaska has had a long and at times stormy relationship with alcohol in general and beer in particular. There are still places in Alaska today where you can be arrested for the mere possession of alcohol or even the ingredients to make homebrew. Bootlegging is alive and well in many remote "dry" communities, with Alaska state troopers routinely arresting individuals for trying to smuggle in alcohol that they bought legally in a store in Anchorage or Fairbanks. For its first thirty years as American soil, all of Alaska was at least theoretically dry, and the citizens of the territory voted to outlaw alcohol in 1916, fully four years before the rest of the nation followed.

Yet despite all the negativity associated with beer and alcohol in the past and even the present, I also learned that Alaska has developed one of the most vibrant and interesting craft beer scenes in America. In 2013, there were 24 breweries and brewpubs, producing 182,530 barrels. That gave Alaska 4.3 craft breweries per 100,000 adults twenty-one and over, which ranked seventh among the fifty states. Alaska produced eleven gallons of craft beer per adult that year, which earned it third place among the other states. While cost and distance make brewers from Alaska reluctant to enter contests, when they do so, they are consistent winners. The bottom line is that the craft beers of Alaska are some of the best brews that almost no one gets to taste who doesn't live here.

So how did this happen? How did a state with a small and scattered population, extreme weather, laughably primitive infrastructure and lousy access to large beer markets manage to bootstrap itself into a craft brewing powerhouse? Well, that's what this book is all about…

Acknowledgements

No book project is the sole creation of its author, especially one involving as much research and as many varied sources as this one. In the course of writing this book, I have been extremely fortunate to receive the unstinting assistance of many different individuals. While I will attempt to catalogue them here, I feel it is almost inevitable that I will overlook someone. If you are that someone and happen to be reading this, please know that your omission was only due to forgetfulness on my part and certainly not from ingratitude.

I would like to recognize and thank my editors at The History Press, first Aubrie Koenig and then her successor Becky LeJeune, for having the confidence in me to offer me this project and then the patience to stick with me as I fumbled my way through it. You were both consummate professionals, and I appreciate all the guidance and assistance you provided me.

Next, I would like to thank Karl Gurcke, the historian of the Klondike Gold Rush National Historical Park. He not only generously spent a significant portion of his valuable time educating me on the historic brewing scene in Skagway and Dyea but also supplied me with an incredibly detailed reference work on the Mascot Saloon, which I have assiduously mined for many of the nuggets you will find in this book.

Another incredibly helpful individual was Sandra M. Johnston of the Alaska State Library Historical Collections, who went to great lengths to aid me in my quest for historical photographs with which to illustrate the first portion of this book. After I had contacted her about obtaining the rights to use certain photos from her library's collection, Ms. Johnston took it upon herself to review several volumes of unpublished photos within the library and found several additional photos that I could also use. Such a generosity of spirit and zest for scholarship deserve all the recognition I can provide in this humble acknowledgement. I am also very grateful for the kind assistance of my friend Jane E. Fuerstenau, the Kenai Peninsula College librarian, who gave me excellent advice on navigating the state library system.

Thanks are also due to Gary J. Klopfer, owner of Snow Goose Restaurant and the Sleeping Lady Brewing Company, and Ray Hodge, formerly of just about every brewery in Alaska at one time or another and currently brewmaster of Blowing Rock Brewing Company in North Carolina. Both of these busy gentlemen were kind enough to spend hours on the phone with me, discussing the events in the brewing world of Alaska in the mid- to late 1990s. I sincerely appreciate their taking the time to talk to me, and I hope my efforts to fit their recollections into an overall narrative meet with their approval.

Special thanks to Geoff and Marcy Larson, owners of Alaskan Brewing Company in Juneau. Not only were they both incredibly generous with their valuable time during the interview process, but they also displayed true Alaskan hospitality to me and my wife, Elaine, during our visit to Juneau. If that were not enough, they generously agreed to supply a foreword to this book. I must also thank Andy Kline and Quinten Hennekam of Alaskan Brewing for supplying some of the more interesting images of the early days at that brewery.

I would also like to express my gratitude to all the other brewers who are quoted in this book; the list is too long to recapitulate here, but to each of you who at one time or another was kind enough to talk to me about brewing craft beer in Alaska, I just want to say thanks, and keep brewing the fantastic beers that make drinking on the Last Frontier such a special pleasure.

I would be remiss if I neglected to thank several of my friends who, each in his own way, encouraged me in this project: Dave Atcheson, Jim Roberts, Tom Dalrymple and Curt Wallace. Thanks for having my back!

Finally, and most importantly, I have to thank the single individual whose support was most critical in turning this book from a vague concept into a concrete reality: my wife, Elaine. She was supportive of what passes for research on a book like this one, i.e., traveling around and drinking beer. Even more importantly, she was willing to generously contribute her time and skill as a photographer, supplying most of the present-day photos that illustrate the latter half of this book. She served as initial proofreader and was a font of good ideas and perceptive advice. It is no exaggeration to say that the book you now hold in your hand would not exist without her being a part of it. Thanks for everything, honey.

Now, let's get started. Cheers!

PROLOGUE

Alaska has always had a peculiar grip on the American imagination. The recent flood of so-called reality TV series set in the state, following the success of *The Deadliest Catch*, demonstrates how fascinating many people today find the Great Land. Yet this is merely the latest incarnation of the spell Alaska has woven over the popular imagination ever since it first burst into America's consciousness during the Klondike gold rush. However, like most such wildly popular ideas, the reality of Alaska bears precious little resemblance to the idealized and romanticized image of popular portrayals.

Unlike many of the residents of the lower forty-eight (typically referred to here as "Outside"), Alaskans know they are living in the heart of an untamed wilderness. Even the residents of Alaska's largest city, Anchorage, must share their streets and neighborhoods with moose and grizzly bears. The rest of the country may hold the comforting belief that nature has been tamed; Alaskans harbor no such illusion. This truly is the Last Frontier, even well into the twenty-first century. Which begs the question: If it is this tough today, what must it have been like in the late nineteenth and early twentieth centuries?

The answer is, of course, tougher, much tougher. The explorers and pioneers who came to Alaska, whether looking for gold, furs, fish or simply new land, were a rough and hardy breed. The anonymous quote used to describe the settlers of the American West is just as accurate in describing the settlers of the American North: "The cowards never started. The weak died on the way. Only the strong arrived. They were the pioneers."

Men and women such as these needed all the help they could get to meet the challenges Alaska would throw at them. And one of the things they needed (and wanted!) most was good beer. In those rough-and-tumble early days, typically the first building in any settlement would have been some combination of trading post and saloon. As a town began to grow, its expansion would be marked by the arrival of the three *B*'s: a bakery, a brothel and a brewery.

All this changed, at least ostensibly, with the coming of Prohibition. But many Alaskans—being the sort of folks who never let the law get in the way of doing what needs to be done—kept right on drinking beer, either imported illegally from Canada or brewed at home. Once the nation realized what a grievous error Prohibition was, legal breweries returned to Alaska, if only for a decade, until the hardships of World War II put the last of them out of business.

For the next thirty-six years, Alaskans made do with beer shipped in from the lower forty-eight or fell back on their old friend: home-brew. Then a group of West German investors decided that the pipeline boom made Anchorage just the place to open a new lager brewery, Prinz Brau. Millions of dollars later, their effort was a bankrupt failure, another costly Alaskan boondoggle, and the idea of brewing a beer in Alaska seemed further away than it had ever been.

Yet as the old saying goes, it's always darkest just before the dawn. Dawn for craft brewing in Alaska came in 1986, when Geoff and Marcy Larson decided to open the Chinook Alaskan Brewing Company in Juneau. Things were touch-and-go several times during the early years, but they persevered, and their eventual success as Alaskan Brewing pointed the way for the many aspiring brewers who have sought to follow in their footsteps.

Since the opening of Chinook Alaskan in 1986, many other breweries and brewpubs have opened in the state; some have been successes, while other have failed for various reasons, but the overall trend has been ever upward. As I write these words, there are twenty-four operating breweries in Alaska, with several more in various stages of planning. Our breweries have won numerous awards in national and international competition, recognizing the outstanding quality of the beers they produce, while Alaskans have become increasingly educated and accepting of craft beer in general and remain fiercely loyal to "their" breweries.

Just like the pioneers who settled this rugged but beautiful land, the craft brewers who are in operation today represent the bravest and the strongest; they are survivors who struggle each and every day to produce outstanding craft beers in some of the harshest and most remote locations on the planet. They are the proud inheritors of over one hundred years of brewing on the Last Frontier, and they are in the process of writing another great chapter.

This book is their story.

PART I
EARLY DAYS (1867 TO 1918)

Chapter 1

THE NEW LAND

The first introduction of alcohol in any form into the area of what is today Alaska was by Russian explorers and fur traders who crossed the Bering Sea in the eighteenth century and "claimed" Alaska in the name of the czar. Russians traded alcohol, along with firearms and other goods, to the indigenous peoples of Alaska for the furs they sought. However, it is clear that from the start the Russian authorities recognized the potential dangers of such activities and sought to control them.

A famous early brewer in Alaskan history was the British explorer Captain James Cook. Aware of the effectiveness of consuming spruce tips to ward off scurvy (thanks to their high vitamin C content), Cook took every opportunity to use them as an ingredient in beers brewed for his crew, likely in lieu of hops. During Cook's third voyage, from 1776 to 1779, he explored and charted much of the coast of Alaska, from Nootka Sound to the Bering Strait, including the Inside Passage and the inlet that today bears his name. During his explorations of the Alaska coastline, his logbook records the production of a spruce tip beer for his crew. However, despite Cook's remarkable achievements, the territory we know as Alaska remained firmly under Russian control.

Aleksandr Andreevich Baranov, governor of Russian Alaska from 1799 to 1818, made extensive efforts to limit the transfer of alcohol and firearms to the local peoples. He was greatly offended whenever other traders willingly sold these items of contraband within his jurisdiction. This concern for keeping alcohol and firearms from Native Alaskans was probably not based on Baranov's feelings about improving the natives' welfare but was simply good business sense, self-preservation and social control. As early as 1808, the Russian government lodged protests with the American consul-general in St. Petersburg against the sale of guns and alcohol to the Alaskan Indians by American merchants. The Russian-American Fur Company set limits on the amount of liquor given their own men as well as to natives. In fact, it was the Russians' rationing that encouraged the British and the Americans to offer alcohol to increase their own trade throughout Russian-America.[1]

The desire to control the alcohol trade with Native Alaskans was not driven by any principled opposition to its consumption. The Russians allowed their workers to brew virtually all the beer that they wanted to drink. The type of beer made was called "kvass" and was consumed freely by all employees. Kvass is a traditional Russian beer brewed from rye bread, with a low alcohol content, typically less than 1.2 percent alcohol by volume (ABV). Even today, kvass is classified as a nonalcoholic drink under Russian and Ukrainian law. Workers also received a small, regular issue of vodka at company expense. This vodka issue was extended to some of the more trusted Aleut hunters at times, particularly at the end of successful hunts.

The major stumbling block for these Russian efforts was the continuing activities of British and American traders in Alaska. Much less concerned with the long-term impact on native communities and much more interested in a quick profit, these traders were eager to trade cheap hard liquor for furs. The Russian government sought a treaty with the United States because foreign competition from these unscrupulous merchants threatened to collapse the Russian-American Fur Company. The United States government was reluctant to interfere with its own merchants just to make things easier on a Russian fur company but eventually agreed. On April 27, 1824, a Russo-American treaty went into effect that allowed American traders in Alaskan waters but prohibited the trading of spirituous liquors, firearms, gunpowder and munitions of war of all kinds. American trading boats were often accused of violating this treaty by the Russians. The treaty, however, did not allow the Russians to seize or even search American vessels suspected of violating the treaty. A similar treaty with the British went into effect in 1825. The Russian-American treaty was not renewed when it expired in 1835 because the American government showed no interest in policing its own trading ships to ensure obedience to it.[2]

With the mounting difficulties faced by their efforts to economically exploit Alaska, it is not surprising that Russia was receptive to the idea of selling the territory when it was approached by the United States. William H.

EARLY DAYS (1867 TO 1918)

Seward, the secretary of state, had been carefully watching events in Alaska after the third charter of the Russian-American Company expired in 1862. When the company declined its renewal offer, the Russian government was faced with the unpleasant prospect of taking over and directly administering the unprofitable and indefensible territory. Following the conclusion of the American Civil War in 1865, it seemed the time might be right to make a deal. Negotiations began in March 1867 and quickly settled on $7 million, plus an additional $200,000 to clear the territory of obligations to the Russian-American Company. Interestingly, one of these obligations was buying out a contract between the company and various breweries in San Francisco, California. Since the 1849 gold rush, the Russian-American Company had been supplying these breweries with ice cut from a pond in Sitka and transported south in ships' holds covered in sawdust! At a final cost of approximately two cents an acre, Russia transferred Alaska and all its accompanying headaches to the United States.[3]

When Alaska became a U.S. territory in 1867, it was declared Indian country in its entirety. At that time, total prohibition throughout Alaska was declared as an extension of U.S. Indian policy dating back to 1834. The prime rationale of this policy was the belief that Indians were dangerous while drinking (at least, they were more dangerous than whites), so prohibition was required to protect the Indians' health and the welfare of whites. The Customs Act, passed in 1868, specifically prohibited the sale, importation and consumption of distilled alcohol in the new territory. The U.S. Army was sent to Alaska to enforce federal law, and according to that law, its members were the only persons legally allowed to possess alcohol within the territory. There was more than a little irony in this, as the post–Civil War army was plagued by drunkenness and desertion. In fact, Alaskan legend has it that a soldier who had deserted from the post at Sitka and "gone Siwash" (a derogatory term for whites who adopted a native-like subsistence lifestyle) first taught Tlingits in the village of Kootznahoo how to make and operate a still. This was the origin of "hoochinoo," the name applied to the crude rum produced by the Tlingits. Hoochinoo was eventually shortened to "hooch" or "hootch," common Alaskan slang for home-brew or moonshine.

As a practical matter, there seems to be little evidence that the army ever attempted to enforce any form of prohibition on non-Indian persons in Alaska. With the transfer of sovereignty, more and more American traders, explorers and prospectors began entering Alaska, and they fully expected to be able to purchase and consume alcohol. In 1874, Levi, Cohen, Fuller & Co. opened in Sitka, then still the territorial capital. The Sitka brewery

Sitka in 1887. *DeGoyler Library Ag.1982.0092.10, Southern Methodist University.*

shipped its product to Tongas, Wrangell, Kodiak, Stickine and other trading posts. This was the first commercial brewer in Alaska, and despite being technically illegal under federal law, it operated successfully until 1900.[4]

The transfer of sovereignty opened vast new territories to exploration by American prospectors, who began flocking to Alaska in search of the next big gold strike. Initially, Sitka served as their base of supply and their focus was on the panhandle region of Southeastern Alaska. Various groups began to explore the lands around the Inside Passage, including two partners by the names of Richard Harris and Joe Juneau. In the summer of 1880, they were hired by a German mining engineer, George Pilz, to explore the region in the vicinity of Holkham Bay. Along with three Tlingit hired as paddlers, Harris and Juneau left Sitka on July 19, 1880. Over the course of that summer, they discovered evidence of gold-bearing ore along a roaring stream pouring into Gastineau Channel, which they promptly named Gold Creek. The discoverers returned to Sitka on November 17, bearing about one thousand pounds of high-grade ore. The first major gold rush in Alaskan history was off and running.

The rush to the Gold Creek region lead to the founding of the town of Juneau, which took its name (after several false starts, including Harrisburgh and Rockwell) from one of its discoverers. Initial deposits of placer gold along Gold Creek and Bullion Creek on nearby Douglas Island played out quickly, but the hard-rock deposits were another matter entirely. While quite

Early Days (1867 to 1918)

Juneau in 1887. *DeGoyler Library Ag.1982.0092.24, Southern Methodist University.*

rich, they could only be exploited through the use of heavy machinery such as stamping mills, unlike placer gold, which could be gathered by men using simple tools such as shovels, gold pans and sluices. As the placer gold played out, the prospectors departed Juneau and the businessmen and mining engineers moved in, men who had the capital and the technical knowledge to pry the gold out of veins in solid rock. Juneau transformed from a camp for prospectors into a town supporting these large-scale mining ventures. As Juneau expanded and began to change from a tent city of itinerant miners into a permanent town supporting the industrial works and stamping mills needed to exploit the nearby gold mines, brewers were quick to recognize a new market. The first brewery was opened in 1886 on Front Street at the corner of Seward Avenue, under the name and ownership of Abraham Cohen. It would operate under various names and owners until 1904. It was joined in 1888 by the U.S. Brewery. Eventually, three of the five largest gold mines in the world were operating concurrently in Juneau, with several breweries there and in nearby Douglas City. Together, they supplied the thirsts of the mine and mill workers in Juneau and the prospectors who now used it as a base of supply to continue their search for gold. Conditions were primitive, but the resourceful brewers made do.

The discovery made by Harris and Juneau proved that there was indeed gold to be found in the Alaskan panhandle and nearby Canadian territories. Now the quest was on to find a truly rich placer deposit, one that would

Beer from Abraham Cohen's Juneau Brewery being delivered by dogcart in 1886. *Alaska State Library P300-122, Capt. George Whitney Photograph Collection.*

allow the average miner working with pick, shovel and pan to reap the reward rather than the man with the capital to bring in heavy machinery. It took another decade, but when that strike was finally made, it began the last great gold rush in American history.

Chapter 2
LOTS OF THIRSTY MEN

In his classic history *The Klondike Fever*, Pierre Berton, whose own father had climbed the Chilkoot Pass in 1898, described that gold rush:

> *The Klondike stampede did not start slowly and build up to a climax, as did many earlier gold rushes. It started instantly with the arrival of the* Excelsior *and* Portland, *reached a fever pitch at once, and remained at fever pitch until the following spring, when, with the coming of the Spanish-American War, the fever died almost as swiftly as it arose. If war had not come, the rush might have continued for another half-year, but even so, the stampede remains unique. It was the last and the most frenzied of the great international gold rushes. Other stampedes involved more gold and more men, but there had been nothing like the Klondike before, there has been nothing like it since, and there can never be anything like it again.*[5]

When word of the gold strike in the Yukon Territory, just across the ill-defined U.S.-Canadian border from Alaska, reached the outside world, the rush it triggered put Alaska into the forefront of the American mind for the first (but not the last) time. Miners who were already in Alaska and had gotten word of the strike in the early fall of 1896 raced to the Klondike, staked their claims on El Dorado Creek and dug gold until the coming of winter froze their diggings. They spent the winter months shivering in their hastily built cabins, subsisting on beans and hardtack, with a fortune in gold and nothing to spend it on. With the coming of spring, they could at last travel via river

ALASKA BEER

Dawson and Klondyke City.

The Klondike Brewery in Dawson City, Yukon Territory. *Alaska State Library P289-221, Sadlier/Olsen Family Photograph Collection.*

steamboats down the mighty Yukon to the port of St. Michael on the Bering Sea and take ships to the lower forty-eight. Two ships carried the first batch of weary but wealthy miners, loaded with gold, to the outside world. The *Excelsior* docked in San Francisco on July 15, 1897, and the *Portland* reached Seattle two days later. When newspapers across the country reported that each ship carried almost two tons of gold, the stampede north was on.

While the wealthiest stampeders could retrace the miners' route and travel the entire way to Dawson City via ship and riverboat, those of lesser means planned to use a more arduous but shorter route: from tidewater over the Chilkoot or White Passes to Lake Bennett, then downstream via raft through various lakes and tributaries, until they reached the Yukon River, which would take them to the goldfields at last. Of course, most of the men and women who started out on this route had only the vaguest idea of the distances and terrain they would need to overcome, and many of them would not complete the journey. Some would lose heart and turn around; other would lose their lives and find instead of gold only a lonely grave somewhere along the way.

Canada lost no time in asserting its sovereignty over the Yukon Territory and its precious gold fields. It did this by the simple expedient of stationing a detachment of the North West Mounted Police at the

Early Days (1867 to 1918)

summits of the Chilkoot and White Passes. Backed up by strategically placed Maxim machine guns, these officers made it clear to the stampeders that they were entering Canadian territory and would be answerable to Canadian law. However, from the summit down to the tidewater was American Alaska, and it was here, on the shores on the Lynn Canal, that two towns sprang up whose names are forever associated with the Klondike Stampede: Dyea and Skagway.

Dyea was the short-lived boomtown at the base of the Chilkoot Pass. Prior to the gold rush, the area was only a seasonal fish camp for the Tlingits, but by the spring of 1897, that began to change. As word of the strike spread, stampeders began to trickle into the area. By that winter, the trickle had turned into a flood as thousands of stampeders slogged through the muddy streets, eating and sleeping in quickly built restaurants and hotels. By 1898, Dyea had outgrown the town plan created only a year before. Dyea's harbor was not as deep as Skagway's, which meant that most ships landed their cargoes at Skagway. Stampeders (including many who had purchased tickets to Dyea) were often left to make their own way over to Dyea and the Chilkoot Pass trail.

Although tens of thousands of people passed through Dyea on their way over the Chilkoot Pass trail, the town's population never exceeded eight thousand. The opening of the White Pass and Yukon Railroad in Skagway meant the end of Dyea. The Chilkoot Pass trail may have been easier or better than the White Pass trail, but it could not compete with both the railroad and the deep-water harbor of its rival town. The town faded away quickly. The post office closed down in 1902. By 1906, the only resident of the town was a man named E.A. Klatt, who abandoned the town after tearing down and burning many of the buildings. Despite its extremely short life span, at one point Dyea boasted three different breweries, all founded in 1898. Both the Alaskan Brewing Company and the Dabzinsky & Babler Brewing Company lasted less than a year, while the George L. Rice & Company managed to hang on until 1904. However, with the rapid decline in Dyea's population, the handwriting was on the wall for all three ventures, almost from the start.

The town of Skagway, Dyea's main competitor for the flood of stampeders, saw the same explosive growth as its rival. Even though the Chilkoot Pass (through Dyea) was the more popular trail, Skagway was always the larger town. The first stampeders arrived in Skagway less than two weeks after the *Portland* had docked in Seattle. On July 29, 1897, when the mail steamer *Queen* landed these first anxious would-be millionaires on the beach, Skagway was barely a collection of tents. By the first half of 1898, when Skagway was teeming with stampeders, it was the biggest town in Alaska. In these wild early days, Skagway was under the control of the notorious con man and crime boss Jefferson Randolph "Soapy" Smith. In her biography of Smith, *King Con,* Jane G. Haigh describes the state of the town:

> *Skagway itself was chaos. Only one dock had been completed so far, and most of the gold seekers and their tons of goods were dumped on the beach. If they could not pack them quickly to higher ground, the inexorable high tides would soon swamp them, ruining sacks of sugar and flour, bacon and beans, and perishable supplies beyond redemption. Beyond the beach, the main street, optimistically named Broadway, was a sea of mud. The businesses lining each side were chiefly saloons and crude hotels, still housed in tents. Billy Moore's sawmill could not keep up with the demand for lumber. And now, hordes of gold seekers were disembarking every day. Heavy snow falling on the summit of White Pass was threatening to close the trail, making all of the new arrivals Soapy's unwilling but welcome hostages for the winter.*[6]

Here was an obvious market for alcohol in all its forms, including beer. If an excuse was needed, there were many to choose from, starting with the absence of sewers and the lack of safe drinking water in Skagway. In addition, it was common knowledge that drinking beer helped prevent scurvy, one of the most common medical threats in the North Country. A large amount of beer was sent north by brewers such as Rainier Brewing of Seattle and the American Brewing Company of St. Louis, Missouri, whose ABC Beer was well known in Skagway. Since beer is 90 percent water and water is the one ingredient for beer that Alaska possesses in abundance, "imports" like Rainier would always be more expensive than locally produced brews. Ads from the time show Rainier selling for twelve and a half cents compared to ten cents for locally produced beer. This price differential shows why local breweries were so quick to open in boomtowns such as Dyea and Skagway.

To meet this demand, three breweries opened in Skagway within three years. Robert Smith and William Matlock founded the Skagway Brewing Company in 1897, hiring Herman Barthel to be their brewmaster. Barthel was a highly respected and experienced brewmaster from San Francisco; hiring such a well-qualified individual signaled the partners' commitment to making a quality product that could compete with the imports from Seattle and elsewhere. Barthel arrived in Skagway in 1898. He was a naturalized

EARLY DAYS (1867 TO 1918)

U.S. citizen, having emigrated from Germany in 1880, and was accompanied by his wife and two sons. Shortly after his arrival, the *Skagway News* began to contain ads for beer from the Skagway Brewing Company, featuring a seated male figure in a tuxedo. A rival newspaper, the *Daily Alaskan*, also contained ads for Skagway Brewing; theirs featured a wrestling bull and lion. Both ads mentioned the brewery's Red Star Beer (possibly inspired by the famous red triangle of Bass Ale—one of the world's first registered trademarks) and solicited "family trade," which referred to beer being purchased for later consumption at home. Clearly, the Skagway Brewing Company was now a going concern.

Given that it was built from scratch, it's not surprising that in 1899 the Skagway Brewery was considered one of the best equipped and thoroughly modern breweries on the Pacific Coast. Its annual capacity was thirty thousand barrels, after an approximately $25,000 investment by Smith and Matlock. Writings at the time describe the building housing the brewery as being four stories tall with walls that were fourteen inches thick and an exterior covered in corrugated iron. The engine and brew room measured thirty feet by thirty feet and contained a thirty-horsepower steam engine that powered the brewery's equipment. Hot and cold running water was piped throughout the building, and the entire structure was heated by steam to maintain the proper brewing temperature throughout the long Alaskan winter. The mash tun was sized to accommodate thirty-barrel batches, and the fermentation cellar had a capacity of eight hundred barrels. There was a large bottling works as well, housed in a separate building.

As large and modern as Skagway Brewing Company was, it still faced competition almost from the start. Charles A. Saake arrived in Skagway in December 1897, accompanied by his wife and two children. Almost immediately, he purchased land for a brewery between Sixth and Seventh Avenues and placed ads in the local papers announcing his intention to open the City Brewery. He then returned to Seattle to purchase the equipment required for the new venture. Saake was an experienced brewer, having worked for the North Pacific Brewing Company, and announced that he intended the City Brewery to produce both lager and steam beer. By the middle of 1900, the City Brewery was well established and providing stiff competition to the Skagway Brewing Company. An article in the *Daily Alaskan* from July of that year describes a visit to Saake's brewery in glowing terms. The City Brewery covered nearly ten thousand square feet and two stories, and every inch was devoted to making beer. Apparently Saake's brewing was a very artisanal process, with him being directly involved in almost every step. The paper reported that the brewery had excellent cold storage rooms, which were kept cool using natural ice, and that City Brewery placed great emphasis on utilizing a proper lagering process. Saake was quoted as reiterating his commitment to Skagway and to making excellent quality steam and lager beers. In what was certainly no coincidence, in the same month that their rival was receiving such a glowing review, Smith and Matlock of Skagway Brewing held an open house and invited the public to come and sample their pure, sparkling lager beer. This beer was described as "clear, amber in color with the most delightful sharp taste…a perfect beer." Smith was quoted describing the quality of his product, and crediting the sophistication of his brewery, stating, "Our plant is perfect." He also bragged about the purity of the brewing water, pumped pure and cold from a depth of fifteen feet.

As if two excellent breweries going head-to-head for the beer trade in Skagway were not enough, for a short period of time, there was a third brewery in the mix: the Gambrinus Brewery, opened by Franz Gansneder in 1898. It was located on Seventh Avenue between Main and State Streets, in the same block as the City Brewery, and also included a bottling plant. Unfortunately, the market in Skagway could not support three large, well-equipped breweries, and the Gambrinus Brewery was the first to falter, going out of business by the fall of 1899.

It should be noted that the establishment of each of these breweries (as well as the saloons they sold their product to) was technically illegal under the territorial law governing Alaska at the time. In 1898, Alaska was still considered Indian country, with the production of alcohol being forbidden by the Customs Act of 1868. However, with stampeders flooding into the territory, it was clear to everyone that a change was needed. In 1899, President William McKinley signed a bill into law that legalized saloons and established an annual $1,500 fee (equivalent to over $35,000 in 2014) for a license to operate, with the funds to be used to support public education. Citizens of Skagway voted to accept this type of licensing scheme as opposed to the alternative, which was to require saloons to submit general petitions from a majority of the (white) adult male and female persons living within a two-mile radius. It had taken over thirty years, but it was at last no longer against the law to produce, sell or consume alcohol in Alaska.

So what were the beers produced by the Skagway breweries (and the other breweries in Alaska that will be discussed in the next chapter) and sold in the town's saloons like? We know from their advertisements that the breweries produced both lager and steam beers. Many of the brewers were emigrants from Germany, where lagers were the dominant beer style, so it's not surprising that they were extremely familiar with producing these beers. Lager beers, of which pilsners or pilseners are the best-known example, are produced using a strain of yeast that works best at low temperatures, typically just a few degrees above freezing. However, the yeast works slowly, meaning the beer must be stored (*lager* is German for "to store") for several weeks at these low temperatures. The end result of this process is a clean-tasting, refreshing brew with a nice malt flavor and crisp hop bitterness. Given the primitive conditions that existed on the rough-and-tumble Western frontier, it was often difficult to achieve the sustained low temperature storage needed for a proper lager. During the early days of the California gold rush in the mid-nineteenth century, brewers in San Francisco were forced to improvise a way to use lager yeast at higher temperatures than normal. The result of their efforts was what came to be known as "steam beer," though exactly why it was given that name remains a matter of debate. Steam beer was (and still is) brewed using a lager yeast but at much higher than normal lager temperatures, resulting in beer that has some of the flavor characteristics of an ale. As many of the brewers who came to Alaska did so by way of stints at breweries on the West Coast, it is not surprising that they would have become familiar with this uniquely American style of beer. Since many of the miners now flocking to the new boomtowns in Alaska also came from that same region, it is again hardly surprising that there was a strong demand for beers made in the style to which they had become accustomed back home. Besides the staples of lager and steam beers, there is also evidence that other beer styles were brewed in Alaska during this period. Porters and stouts were advertised and seemed to have been quite popular, as well as other British styles, such as imitators of the famous Bass Ale. Of particular interest is a German-style altbier, brewed by the Douglas City Brewing Company near Juneau in 1907; we will learn more about this beer and its remarkable recreation in chapter 8.

Despite the desires of the breweries to establish the "family trade," with their beers being purchased for consumption at home, the vast majority of their product was sold in the saloons of Skagway. What were these saloons like? In the earliest days of the gold rush, they would have been primitive in the extreme. In August 1897, Tappan Adney was covering the stampede for *Harper's Weekly*. Describing the tent saloons of Skagway, he wrote, "A glimpse inside these as one rides by shows a few boards set up for a bar in one corner, the other corners being filled with gambling layouts, around which crowds of men are playing or looking on."[7]

Alaska Beer

At the time Adney passed through Skagway, at the very start of the stampede, there were only four such tent saloons in operation: the Pack Train, the Grotto, the Bonanza and the Nugget. By Christmas of 1897, there were some 27 saloons in operation, and the number continued to grow. In late March and early April 1898, U.S. customs agents in Dyea and Skagway raided 120 of the saloons, hotels and restaurants serving liquor between the tidewater and the Canadian border, as the manufacture, sale or possession of alcohol was still illegal. Some 35 saloons in Skagway appear on the list of establishments raided. By mid-summer of 1898, which witnessed the famous demise of Soapy Smith in a shootout on July 8 with Frank Reid at the Juneau Company Wharf, it is estimated that there were over 50 saloons operating in Skagway. By the spring of 1899, there were 80. These saloons were no longer the crude tent structures from the summer and fall of 1897 described by Tappan Adney; they were solidly constructed buildings with comfortable, even luxurious interiors. Thanks to extensive historical and archaeological research, perhaps the best documented of any of these saloons is the Mascot. It was Skagway's longest, most enduring saloon under single management at the same location. Founded in April 1898 as the Mascotte by Charles Rohbak and now a part of the Klondike Gold Rush National Historical Park, the Mascot is located on the corner of Broadway and Third Avenue. It has been restored as closely as possible to its appearance circa 1905 to 1916.

In early 1899, when the new licensing law came into force requiring Skagway saloons to pay a $1,500 license fee in order to remain open, many saloons were unable to afford the fee. Of the eighty saloons reported operating in January 1899, only a dozen remained by April. Charles Rohbak's Mascotte saloon was one of those that closed. On June 13, 1899, Charles Saake, the owner of the City Brewery, and Albert Reinert, a thirty-two-year-old recent arrival from Seattle, purchased the saloon. After they acquired the building and saloon fixtures, they paid the license fee, remodeled the interior and reopened as the Mascot. Alterations and improvements were made, and Reinert moved into the upstairs apartment. By all accounts, Albert Reinert was a congenial host. A former restaurant owner, his popular free lunches varied from clam chowder to spareribs and sauerkraut to Mexican enchiladas. Saake supplied the saloon with his locally brewed pilsner beer, which went for a nickel a schooner. Its staff of bartenders was considered "hail fellows." One notable character was Ham Grease Jimmy. According to legend, he was a bartender at the Mascot until a lucky chip on the right number earned him enough to buy his own saloon, White Pass City's largest. Another bartender, Chris Shea, later became Skagway's mayor.

Despite the apparent success of the Mascot, trouble arose between Saake and Reinert. In order to dissolve their partnership, they decided to auction the Mascot to the highest bidder. On May 23, 1901, City Marshal Snook rolled a beer barrel out front and auctioned off the saloon. The highest bidder was Albert Reinert at $6,025. Reinert then began another extensive remodeling and enlargement program. The east wall was removed, and the building was doubled in length. A new plate glass façade went in. Telegraph wires were installed, a possible move to get direct reports on sporting events. In 1903, Reinert installed a Victor Talking Machine and advertised an electric concert every night. By 1905, the building reached its present configuration when the corner entry was removed and a new plate glass front and central double-door entry was installed. This was a "males only" establishment. Women and minors were not allowed in saloons, a restriction dictated by Alaska law. Located on "Steamboat Row" (named for the numerous steamship companies' offices in the area), the Mascot continued to be popular. Serving longshoremen and others, however, sometimes proved troublesome. Fighting, pulling pistols or throwing stones through the plate-glass windows were some of the incidents reported in the local press. Still,

Celebrating the grand reopening of Skagway's Mascot Saloon on August 14, 1904. Front and center is Albert Reinert, proud owner. *George and Edna Rapuzzi Collection.*

the Mascot remained a successful Skagway saloon for over a decade; few of its competitors could say the same.

Even with the end of the stampede in 1898, workers continued to flood into Skagway to work on the construction of the White Pass and Yukon Route Railroad. Despite the expense of the annual license fee from 1899, it appears the saloon numbers in Skagway remained at relatively high levels until the completion of the route on July 29, 1900. Then the bottom fell out of the saloon business in Skagway. As the saloons fell on hard times, so did the breweries that supplied them. During 1900 to 1901, business became very competitive between the breweries and local saloons, thanks to the decreasing single male population of Skagway. Skagway's economy was no longer growing, and it was becoming increasingly clear that it was not going to become a northern metropolis. The beer market was shrinking, and the sale of "import beers" such as Rainier at local saloons provided strong competition to local breweries. It is possible that this may have been the source of the conflict between Saake and Reinert at the Mascot, since after obtaining sole ownership, Reinert began offering Rainier's beers rather than Saake's local products. Rainier was certainly very aggressive in promoting its products and ran weekly ads in the local paper, promoting its beer as a "pure food." Smith and Matlock of the Skagway Brewing Company were also very unhappy that the local breweries did not receive the support of the local saloons. Smith sought to have the local saloons carry only his beer and repeatedly ran ads in the local paper that asked the question, "Do you patronize home industry?"

These ads by Robert Smith are the first example of a theme that will recur again and again throughout the history of brewing in Alaska: the call for consumers to support local, as opposed to Outside, breweries. The goal of the appeal is to convince Alaskans to spend their money within the territory (or since 1959, the state), in order to help its economy and put Alaskans to work. Such appeals had little traction with the average consumer in Skagway when Robert Smith first made them in 1900, but as we shall see later in this history, by the late twentieth century and early twenty-first, they were powerful indeed. But all that was still far in the future, and Smith was forced to grapple with the challenges of his own time. In July 1901, he traveled north, hoping to find distributors for his beer in Dawson, Whitehorse and Aitlin. The *Daily Alaskan* newspaper reported that he had a very successful trip, with one hundred barrels of beer to be forwarded to a consignee in Dawson. Yet for a brewery capable of producing thirty thousand barrels a year, selling less than two days production must have been a disappointment. Smith and Matlock began to look to cut their losses.

By the end of 1901, there had been a serious shakeup in the brewing business in Skagway. The City Brewery ceased operation; Charles Saake remained in Skagway but changed his profession from brewer to saloonkeeper, continuing his rivalry with his former partner Albert Reinert. Robert Smith and William Matlock sold the Skagway Brewing Company to its brewmaster, Herman Barthel; the 1902 business license for the brewery lists him as the sole owner. Smith and Matlock left Skagway to pursue other business interests around the territory, though they both retained properties in the town. By the fall of 1902, Skagway had only seven saloons still operating. The high license fee and decreasing population were draining resources faster than saloonkeepers could bring in customers. Skagway's saloon owners instituted a custom that had long been practiced in the rest of the country but had not been necessary during the gold rush days: the free lunch. Starting in October, as the summer transients left town, all of the saloons engaged in a bitter warfare to see who could offer the swankiest free meal, while keeping their drink prices high. It was another sign that the saloon business in Skagway was becoming increasingly cutthroat and did not bode well for the future.

A tough economy was not the only threat faced by the saloons and the one remaining brewery in Skagway. Besides a shrinking customer base and competition from Outside breweries, Herman Barthel's Skagway Brewing had to contend with the growing calls for prohibition, spearheaded by the local chapter of the Women's Christian Temperance Union (WCTU). The first mention of the WCTU in Skagway appeared on April 15, 1900, when the *Daily Alaskan* announced a meeting at the home of one of its members. The president of the local chapter was Mrs. Sarah E. Shorthill, a woman in her fifties who had been a member of the WCTU for eighteen years. Under her leadership, it was not long before the local chapter began pushing for reform in Skagway. On September 22, 1900, it filed a protest against the issuance of licenses to the Reception, Senate, Seattle and Fifth Avenue saloons, based on a territorial law forbidding saloons from having an entrance within four hundred feet of a church or school. After a bruising public fight, a judge declared that two of the four saloons were greater than four hundred feet from the church in question, and one had reopened a different entrance to come into compliance, leaving only the Reception to be denied a license. However, the main impact of the WCTU action seemed to be to delay the construction of a new public school in Skagway (funded by saloon license fees), since the proposed site was also within four hundred feet of several saloons. A few months later, Mrs. Shorthill resigned from the local chapter and left

Skagway. The other members of the local WCTU chapter were apparently embarrassed by the whole affair, as the chapter immediately disbanded.

If the saloonkeepers breathed a sigh of relief, it was short-lived. The reformers fighting for a "moral" Alaska resumed their attack in mid-1903, when District Attorney John Boyce brought a protest against the issuance of liquor licenses to Skagway saloons, which had, in the past, opened their doors on Sunday. Five saloons promptly closed their doors on Sunday, and the rest followed suit soon after. Women were also completely barred from saloons, causing difficulties for owners such as Albert Reinert who catered to the family trade of selling for home consumption. Reinert's solution was to install a telephone at the Mascot, allowing women to phone in orders for delivery to their home.

Herman Barthel did his best to maintain the Skagway Brewing Company as a going concern, but the combination of economics and moralists was eventually too much for him. The Skagway Brewing Company closed its doors in 1905. In June 1906, William Matlock, one of the founders of the Skagway Brewing Company, attempted to resurrect brewing in Skagway by providing funding to William Schwartzenberg, another German-born brewer who had come to the United States in 1891. In August, Schwartzenberg began advertising his new business, the Eagle Brewery. It's unclear exactly how long the brewery operated; some sources indicate it was in business until 1910, but no advertisements appear for it in the local papers after October 1906. It was certainly defunct by 1913, when Matlock filed a civil action against Schwartzenberg to recover the money owed to him, since by then Schwartzenberg was residing outside Skagway at the Perseverance Mine in Juneau.

So ends the story of brewing in Skagway, for the next nine decades. Like the miners looking for gold, we must head much farther north for the next chapter in the history of beer in Alaska.

Chapter 3
GOLD FIELDS

When the stampeders finally began to flood into Dawson City in the late spring and summer of 1898, expecting to make their fortune from the gold fields, they were sorely disappointed. All the potential claims along both the El Dorado and Bonanza Creeks had been staked many months before by prospectors who were already in Alaska and had gotten news of the strike long before it reached the outside world and triggered the rush. Just about the only work available for the newcomers was digging for hire on another man's claim, which was hardly the dream they had struggled and sacrificed so much for. For many, this disappointment meant the end of their romance with the North Country; after seeing the sights of Dawson City, they retraced their steps, returning over the passes to Skagway, where they took passage home. While they were no richer in dollars, they now had a wealth of stories about their adventures during the great Klondike gold rush, stories they could tell their children and grandchildren for the rest of their lives.

But for many of the stampeders, going home was not an option. Perhaps they had nothing to return to or perhaps they were just too stubborn to admit defeat. For whatever reason, these individuals chose to remain in the territory and continue to seek their fortunes. Some found work on the White Pass and Yukon Route railroad, which was wending its way from Skagway to Whitehorse. Others drifted around the backcountry of Alaska, from mining camp to mining camp, hoping to get in on the ground floor of the next big strike. In the summer of 1899, word of mouth sent them all scurrying west down the Yukon River, heading for a town with the unusual name of Nome. Cape Nome, the geographic feature on the Seward Peninsula from which the future town would take its name, apparently earned that appellation via a clerical error. The cape had been noted on Russian charts as Mys Sredniy (Cape Middle) but seems to have received its English name when a draftsman in the British Admiralty mistook the query "? name" on a draft chart to be "C. Nome" or Cape Nome. He inscribed his error on the chart he produced, and the name has been carried forward ever since.[8]

The first discoveries at Nome took place in September 1898, with claims being staked along the Anvil Creek by the so-called three lucky Swedes: John Brynteson, Eric O. Lindblom and Jafet Lindeberg. Besides being lucky, the discoverers were also shrewd, or perhaps devious, if you prefer. Using powers of attorney, they filed forty-three claims in their own names and forty-seven in the names of others, including L.B. Shepherd, the U.S. commissioner in nearby St. Michael, and Captain E.S. Walker, the commander of the troops stationed there. When newcomers attempted to challenge the legality of the claims, Shepherd ruled in favor of the Swedes (and himself) while Walker called out his troops to enforce Shepherd's decision. This blatant corruption was immortalized in Rex Beach's 1906 novel, *The Spoilers*. Beach was a miner in Nome during the period in question and witnessed firsthand the events, which he later fictionalized. The court cases that resulted from the claims along Anvil Creek dragged on for years, with one case going on for twenty years, involving eleven different courts and being ruled on by the U.S. Supreme Court four times.[9]

Nome was only a short trip by boat across Norton Sound from St. Michael. By the spring of 1899, many passengers who arrived there en route to the Klondike changed their destination to Nome. Other miners, returning empty-handed down the Yukon from Dawson, decided to give Nome a try before giving up and leaving Alaska for good. Miners from all across the territory began to arrive in Nome, only to find that every conceivable claim had already been staked by the Swedes. The situation was rapidly becoming explosive, with the frustrated miners on one side and Captain Walker's troops on the other. What saved the district from insurrection and total anarchy was the discovery in the summer of 1899 that there was gold on the beaches on Nome. Unlike gold in the rivers and creeks that had to be sluiced, or gold held tightly by the permafrost that had to be chipped and thawed, or gold trapped in ore that had to be milled, this was free gold in the black sand of the beaches. All that was needed was a shovel and something to sift with. Since placer gold like this was as good as currency and could be taken straight from the ground to the bank, a prospector might as well have been picking up coins. While no one became a millionaire on the beach, it provided a much-needed safety valve.

Compared to the Klondike and other strikes in the interior of Alaska, Nome was relatively easy to reach, as the entire trip could be made by boat. Coupled with the easy pickings on the beach, this fueled an explosive growth. By the early fall of 1899, there were at least three thousand inhabitants, and some estimate that over five thousand spent the winter of 1899–1900 there. Gamblers, saloonkeepers, merchants and prostitutes flocked there from all over Alaska and the western United States. The most well known of these was Wyatt Earp, already famous for his participation in the gunfight at the OK Corral in Tombstone, Arizona, in 1881. Earp and his wife, Josephine, had spent the last two decades traveling around the West, chasing one boom after another, always looking for quick and easy money. In September 1899, the Earps arrived in Nome, where Wyatt, along with his partner, Charles E. Hoxie, built the Dexter Saloon, the city's first two-story wooden building and its largest and most luxurious saloon, some seventy feet by thirty feet with twelve-foot ceilings. The second floor had twelve "clubrooms" decorated with fine mirrors, thick carpets, draperies and sideboards. Despite the sophisticated-sounding name, in reality Earp ran the second floor as a brothel.

While there might be a nice saloon (and brothel) in Nome, conditions there were anything but healthy. No one wanted to dig cesspools when they could be digging gold, so deaths from typhoid were common. Once again, a lack of clean drinking water put a premium on safe substitutes, such as beer. Two breweries opened in Nome in 1900 to meet this need, the Alaskan Brewing Company and the Cape Nome Brewing and Trading Company. Neither lasted more than a year. However, in 1901 Henry Kern paid a $500 licensing fee and opened the Nome Brewing & Bottling Company on D Street near Dry Creek. Finally, the citizens of Nome had a source for locally produced beer. This brewery would remain in business until 1915, when it was closed by the coming of local prohibition to Nome.

Through the next several years, Nome grew and developed into a bustling city with remarkable speed. By 1905, Nome had twenty-five thousand inhabitants and paved, electrically lighted thoroughfares lined with banks, schools, churches and theaters. The city boasted a telephone system, a telegraph to the outside and three separate railroad lines. Its residents could read about local events in three daily newspapers and even enjoy fresh vegetables from a substantial number of greenhouses. Such growth meant good business for the local brewery, though the ease of shipping to Nome

Olympia Beer being unloaded by lighter in Nome on June 16, 1908. *O.D. Goetze, O.D. Goetze Collection; Anchorage Museum, B2001.041.185.*

meant they still faced substantial competition from West Coast breweries, such as Olympia from Seattle, Washington. This sort of competition was at its most fierce in those port towns where shipping from the West Coast was the cheapest. For example, Skagway was a major shipping port, with freight moving from the harbor via the White Pass and Yukon Railroad to Whitehorse and then on the Dawson; we saw in the last chapter how difficult this made it for local breweries to survive there. Another example would be Seward, founded in 1903 as the ice-free port for the southern terminus of the Alaska Railroad. Seward was one of the few towns in Alaska that had no local brewery in the early twentieth century. That is not to say that there was no beer in Seward. On the contrary, there was plenty of beer, all of which was brewed on the West Coast and shipped there, along with the railroad equipment.

All across Alaska, the pattern would be repeated, with towns springing up in response to gold strikes. In some cases, such as in Nome or Juneau, the strike would be of sufficient magnitude that the town (along with its

Olympia Beer from Seattle is featured at the Commerce Bar in Seward, Alaska. *Alaska State Library P349-135, Feaster Family Photograph Collection.*

Interior of the Cohen Brewery in Juneau, circa 1900. The figure on the right is believed to be the owner, Marcus J. Cohen. *Alaska State Library Juneau-Breweries-12, Alaska State Library Photograph Collection.*

Exterior of the Eagle Brewing Company in Juneau, circa 1905. *Alaska State Library Juneau-Breweries-14, Alaska State Library Photograph Collection.*

Bottle label for the Eagle Brewing Company. *Alaska State Library MS108-1-02, Labels Used on Alaska-Related Products Manuscript Collection.*

brewery) would achieve a degree of permanence. Juneau, which became the territorial capital in 1906 instead of Sitka, supported its first brewery, the Cohen Brewery, for almost twenty years from 1886 to 1904. The brewery was quite a substantial affair, judging by the surviving photographs.

Equally long-lived was another Juneau brewery, which opened in 1899 under the name Matlock Brewing Company. This company had four different names in its lifetime, becoming the Juneau Alaska Brewing and Malting Company in 1900, the Eagle Brewing Company in 1904, and the Alaska Brewing and Malting Company in 1906. Regardless of changes in names and proprietorship, it remained in business until closed by territorial prohibition in 1918, indicating its economic viability.

Still, things almost always began fairly primitively in Alaska. Take the Valdez Brewing & Bottling Works, founded by a Mr. A.M. Edwards and a Dr. Von Gunther, as an example. Valdez, an ice-free port on Prince William Sound, was the gateway to the country around Copper Center. It is famous for the enormous amount of snow it receives each winter. In the winter of 1898 to 1899, thousands of prospectors stranded in the cluster of tents that was Valdez suffered terribly from starvation and scurvy before being rescued by a detachment of the U.S. Army in the spring. That detachment proceeded to construct a military road north to Fairbanks, the forerunner of today's Richardson Highway. With a new road and its ice-free port, Valdez became permanently established as the first overland supply route into the interior of Alaska. The brewery was established in 1903 in conditions for which "primitive" might be a generous term. Yet no matter how primitive things might have started out, typically if a town prospered, its brewery would also prosper. The Valdez Brewing and Bottling Works moved to new site in 1909 and continued to grow and expand until 1918, when it, too, was closed down by territorial prohibition.

Compare the longevity of these breweries with the three breweries that opened in Circle City on the Yukon in the boom year of 1899; by 1900, every one had shut its doors. Or the Eureka Brewing Company of Fort Wrangell, which was born in 1898 and closed a year later, leaving only its ads behind.

Still, even in Fort Wrangell, a brewery could be successful. The Fort Wrangell Brewery was founded in 1891 by Henry Uhler on Front Street. He operated it until his death in 1895, at which point it was purchased from his estate by a Mr. Bruno Greif, who operated it until 1902. Greif sold his keg beer sold for $0.40 a gallon, with bottled beer costing $1.50 per dozen. His advertisements referred to his establishment as a "Beer Hall and Lunch Bar,"

BREWERY AND BOTTLING WORKS.
VALDEZ, ALASKA.

Remember the

Eureka Brewing Co.

432 FRONT STREET,

Fort Wrangel, Alaska.

A nice cozy place to spend an afternoon or evening.

Best Refreshments in the City.

Newspaper ad for the short-lived Eureka Brewing Co. of Fort Wrangell. *Alaska State Library Advertisements-Alaskan-04, Alaska State Library Photograph Collection.*

Opposite, top: First location of the Valdez Brewing and Bottling Works, circa 1903. *Crary-Henderson Collection; Anchorage Museum, Gift of Ken Hinchey, B1962.001.1736.*

Opposite, bottom: New location for the Valdez Brewing & Bottling Works, circa 1909. *P.S. Hunt, Crary-Henderson Collection; Anchorage Museum, Gift of Ken Hinchey, B1962.001A.248.*

suggesting that his brewery was much like one of our modern brewpubs. Greif also made an appeal to buy Alaskan, with the slogan "Patronize Home Industry and You Will Be Happy."

Why the emphasis on buying Alaskan? The Fort Wrangell Brewery faced the same sort of competitive pressures as breweries in Skagway and Nome from beer being shipped in from the West Coast. For example, just down the street from that brewery was the Cassiar, a bar that served beers from breweries in Seattle. There was even a large sign out front reading "Brewery," with the words "Seattle Beer" in small print. Smaller signs indicate that the bar served beers from both Rainier and Olympia Breweries. With competition like that, it becomes obvious why Greif tried to invoke local loyalty in his potential customers.

One of the final big gold rushes in the history of Alaska led to the founding of Fairbanks, at the juncture of the Yukon and Tanana Rivers. The first strikes were made late in the summer of 1903, and by 1904, travelers headed up the Yukon to Dawson began detouring to Fairbanks, recognizing that the latter was the more booming town. Fairbanks developed into the supply hub for several mining camps in the hills north, places with names like Pedro Camp, Livengood, Fox, Gilmore, Olnes and Chatanika. It was

The Fort Wrangell Brewery, circa 1900. *Alaska Sate Library Wrangell Businesses-6, Alaska State Library Photograph Collection.*

Opposite, top: Newspaper ad for the Fort Wrangell Brewery, circa 1900. *Alaska State Library Advertisements-Alaskan-03, Alaska State Library Photograph Collection.*

Opposite, bottom: The Cassiar Bar in Wrangell on June 4, 1908. *Alaska State Library P226-386, William Norton Photograph Collection.*

slow in starting, but by the end, the boom at Fairbanks was likely the most profitable of all the Alaskan strikes, with estimates of $63 million in gold produced from area mines. At 2014 prices, that would be the equivalent of $3.78 billion. To meet the demand for beer in Fairbanks, two breweries

opened, both in 1905. The first was the Barthel Brewing Company, under the ownership of Herman Barthel, who we first met as the brewmaster then owner of Skagway Brewing Company. When the twin forces of competition from West Coast imports and local prohibitionists became too much for him in Skagway, Barthel moved on to the new city of Fairbanks. Using the expertise he'd gained in Skagway, he made his new brewery into a successful business, one that operated from 1905 until the coming of territorial prohibition in 1918.

Barthel's competition for the Fairbanks beer market came from the Tanana Brewing Company, which was located on Second Avenue in the new city. Unlike Barthel's brewery, this company had a much more difficult time of it, changing its name and owners twice before finally going out of business. In 1906, it reorganized as the Fairbanks Brewing Company and then in 1907 became the Arctic Brewing Company. In 1910, the brewery closed its doors permanently, leaving Herman Barthel firmly in charge of the market for locally brewed beer in Fairbanks.

Given its dominant position in modern Alaska, both in terms of population and economic clout, one might wonder why there has been no mention of the city of Anchorage so far in this history. In point of fact, Anchorage is a relative latecomer on the Alaskan scene. Founded in 1915 to support the construction of the Alaskan Railroad from Seward to Fairbanks, Anchorage remained essentially a railroad company town until the military build-up during and after World War II. Because of its late start and small size, Anchorage never had a brewery prior to the establishment of territorial prohibition in 1918. Indeed, the first brewery would not be built in Anchorage until 1976, and even that one would fail within three years. Still, with a few exceptions such as Seward and Anchorage, almost every town of substance founded during the gold rush era in Alaska would have at least one and often multiple breweries. From 1874 until 1918, thirty-two different breweries operated in fourteen different cities and towns in Alaska. Yet, in spite of their important role in helping to settle and develop the Last Frontier, every one of these businesses would be closed by 1918. The Noble Experiment had come to Alaska.

Part II
Dry Spell
(1918 to 1976)

Chapter 4
Bone Dry

Why Prohibition? Scholars continue to ask that question to this day. The idea of outlawing a substance that had been enjoyed by a large segment of the population since time immemorial seems a strange one to be adopted by popular vote in a country as freedom-loving as the United States. It seems even more so in a territory as fiercely individualistic as Alaska. From its ratification in 1789 through its first seventeen amendments, the Constitution of the United States had always limited the power of the government, never of its citizens, with only one exception. With ratification of the Eighteenth Amendment, there were now two exceptions: citizens couldn't own slaves and couldn't buy alcohol. In Alaska, territorial prohibition went into effect even earlier, on January 1, 1918. As of that date, the Territory of Alaska was, at least in theory, bone dry with regards to alcohol.

What were the forces that led to prohibition in Alaska? On the national stage, there were two major organizations advocating for prohibition. The first of these was the National Women's Christian Temperance Union (WCTU), founded in Cleveland, Ohio, in 1874. During the winter of 1873–74, groups of women in towns across New York and Ohio began to engage in nonviolent protests against the sale of alcohol. These protests were typically inspired by a lecture on the evils of drink, after which the formerly quiet housewives would occupy local saloons by praying on their knees and demanding that all liquor sales cease. It came to be known as the "Woman's Crusade," and it succeeded in removing legal liquor sales from some 250 communities. Heartened by these successes, the participants founded the WCTU under the slogan "For God and Home and Native Land" (later changed to "Every Land"). The WCTU selected the white ribbon bow as its symbol, and its watchwords were "Agitate-Educate-Legislate." The WCTU asked individuals to pledge total abstinence from alcohol, tobacco and other drugs. Its members were primarily motivated by the threats to home and family they believed were posed by these substances. As mentioned in chapter 2, the first chapter of the WCTU in Alaska organized in early 1900 in Skagway, with Sarah Shorthill as its president.

The other major national organization promoting prohibition was the Anti-Saloon League. Founded as a state society in 1893 in Oberlin, Ohio, the Anti-Saloon League became a nation organization under the brilliant guidance of Wayne B. Wheeler. He built it into the first single-issue political organization in American history. For the league, all that mattered about a politician was whether he was "wet" or "dry," i.e., did he vote for or against the prohibition of alcohol. Even politicians who privately consumed alcohol, were corrupt or had other unsavory personal habits were supported by the league, so long as they voted reliably dry. By the second decade of the twentieth century, the Anti-Saloon League was the premiere prohibitionist organization in the United States.

Of these two organizations, in Alaska, the WCTU was clearly much more influential. While the Anti-Saloon League also participated in state and local politics, Alaska was far away and never a high priority. By contrast, the WCTU was built around local chapters, whose members were in the best position to both observe the evils of the saloons in their towns and agitate against them. Alaskan women were also more effective in their efforts for another reason: unlike most of the rest of the United States, the women of Alaska could vote.

For decades, women's groups in the United States (including prominently the WCTU) had fought for the right to vote, making the most headway in the American West. Rather than directly grant Alaska's women the right to vote, Congress gave that power to the Alaska legislature when it approved the law creating the Territory of Alaska, signed by President Taft on August 24, 1912. When the first territorial legislature met, its first act was to unanimously approve a bill to allow women to vote. Legislators said that women had proven themselves in Alaska and had done much to support its development. Others believed that allowing women to vote was important because it would increase the number of voters, which would impress government officials who questioned the stability and the future of Alaska. Senator Henry Roden of Iditarod said it was an easy issue to deal with because it did not "cost any member anything, nor their friends." At that time, only nine states (Idaho, Wyoming, Utah, Colorado, Washington, California, Oregon, Arizona and Kansas) had granted women the vote.

The women who joined the WCTU chapters in Skagway and elsewhere in Alaska were concerned by what they saw as the three evils endemic to the saloon: alcohol, gambling, and prostitution. In their worldview, the stereotypical bad husband (never their own man, of course) would take his paycheck to the saloon in order to drink, gamble and sleep with a syphilitic prostitute. Then he would return to his poor family, unable to feed his children and primed to infect his wife with a horrible disease. It was the fervent desire to save society from these perceived horrors that motivated these morally upright women to do their utmost to outlaw the saloon's reason for existing: the sale of alcohol.

Were the saloons of Alaska truly that bad? As with most complex questions, the answer to that seems to be "it depends." We will use Skagway as an example, since that town has some of the longest and most complete records. In its earliest days, from the start of the Klondike gold rush to the institution of the $1,500 license fee on July 1, 1899, such a characterization of the saloon as dens of vice was likely spot on, at least with respect to the first two vices: alcohol and gambling. With regard to the third, prostitution, it's difficult to distinguish between brothels that offered alcohol and saloons that offered prostitution. After the establishment of the license fee, most of the smaller, more squalid saloons went out of business, and the city eventually established a red-light district for brothels on Seventh Avenue, between State and Broadway Avenues. As the number of saloons fell and the investment by the owners in them increased, the tolerance of those owners for any sort of illegal activity on their premises also decreased sharply. Any gambling or prostitution occurring on licensed premises put the annual renewal of that license at risk and, along with it, the saloonkeeper's livelihood. This is not to say that Skagway was bereft of gambling or prostitution— far from it. One of the major sources of revenue for the government of Skagway (and that of many other frontier towns, both in the lower forty-eight and Alaska) was the fines levied on "illegal" gambling and prostitution. The Skagway Magistrate Dockets shows that from 1903 to 1906, the court received $3,417.00 in fines from prostitutes, $3,007.60

in fines from gamblers and \$1,087.00 from all other fines combined.[10] These fines amounted to a de facto tax by the town on these activities; for professional gamblers and whores, it was simply part of the cost of doing business. So while there was clearly plenty of gambling and prostitution happening in Skagway, it appears that little of it was actually taking place in saloons. However, since women were barred from saloons by city ordinance (and no respectable woman would consider entering one, lest she be branded a whore), it's likely that the members of the Skagway chapter of the WCTU had very little idea what actually went on inside these male-only spaces. In fact, during an eighty-one-month period, for nine saloons in Skagway, there were only thirty-three crimes reported, most of them minor acts of larceny or drunken brawls between patrons. This hardly supports the image of the wild-and-wooly frontier saloon from popular fiction or the squalid dens of vice imagined by the upright ladies of Skagway.

The Skagway chapter of the WCTU disbanded in late 1900 after the embarrassing fiasco discussed in chapter 2. The organization did not reappear in Skagway until September 1908, when a Ketchikan resident by the name of Mrs. Conner helped to organize a new branch there. Initially, the newly reconstituted branch seemed to eschew any attacks on the saloons, focusing instead on the betterment of the community by working on such projects as the demolition of unsightly shacks, improvement in local sanitary condition and the school grounds and the erection of a public drinking fountain for horses and dogs. Inevitably, however, the Skagway chapter eventually renewed its war on saloons. This time around, the battle would be fought in a different arena: at the ballot box. In the election of 1914 in Skagway, the first after women were granted the vote the previous year, they promptly voted out the longtime city council and the incumbent three-term mayor, Josiah M. Tanner, replacing them with a city government sympathetic to their views. Then on June 6, 1915, a special election was held in Skagway on the issue of local prohibition. The WCTU made a maximum effort; many voters were brought to the polls in a horse-drawn wagon bearing the sign "Vote Dry and Protect Your Home." The final results were a clear victory for the WCTU with 193 votes in favor to 153 against; Skagway had voted itself dry. The town's five operating saloons were given until August 21 to dispose of their remaining stocks. Still, the anti-alcohol forces were not unstoppable; in similar elections that year, Haines, Juneau, Ketchikan and Petersburg all voted to continue issuing saloon licenses.

Dry Spell (1918 to 1976)

In light of these special elections in 1915, the two-year-old Alaska territorial legislature decided to ask Alaskans whether they wanted a territorial ban on the sale and manufacture of liquor. The United States as a whole was moving toward approving the Eighteenth Amendment, and the same forces were at play in Alaska. "The prohibition cause seems to be gaining rapidly in Alaska and it is my opinion that prohibition will be carried as soon as we can get a fair expression of the voice of the people of this territory," territorial governor John Strong wrote in 1915. He also believed that granting women the right to vote in 1913 had been critical in the campaign against alcohol. "To the votes of the women of Alaska may be ascribed the crystallization of public sentiment against the liquor traffic in the territory," he said.

In November 1916, this advisory vote took place, with the anti-alcohol forces triumphing by more than a two-to-one margin. While the vote was closer than that in most urban areas, the only places in Alaska that didn't vote to go dry were Eagle, St. Michael and the nearly abandoned town of Chena, near Fairbanks. However, Congress still retained ultimate authority over Alaska, so its approval would be required. Alaskan congressional delegate James Wickersham arranged to introduce a bill in Congress on January 23, 1917, to implement the provisions of the November vote. Wickersham said at the time that the anti-liquor sentiment was due to dissatisfaction with the way saloons were being run; they were regarded as a "menace to many people." In what seems like a remarkably rapid fashion to political watchers today but was probably due to pressure from Wheeler's Anti-Saloon League, the bill passed Congress and was signed into law on February 14, 1917, by President Woodrow Wilson. Called the "Alaska Bone Dry Law," this bill stated that "it shall be unlawful for any person, house, association, firm, company, club, or corporation, his, its, or their agents, officers, clerks, or servants, to manufacture, sell, give, or otherwise dispose of any intoxicating liquor or alcohol of any kind in the Territory of Alaska, or to have in his or its possession or to transport any intoxicating liquor or alcohol in the Territory of Alaska." The bill provided only three allowable exceptions: wine to be used for sacramental purposes, medicinal alcohol to be dispensed by pharmacists or pure alcohol for scientific, artistic or mechanical purposes. Each exception came with a stringent approval process and a large amount of required documentation. This new law took effect on January 1, 1918.

Alaskan voters had embraced Prohibition by a large margin, putting out of business all the breweries and saloons in the territory, at least in theory. Just over two years later, on January 16, 1920, the rest of the United States decided it would follow the Last Frontier into the uncharted waters of the Noble Experiment. Almost immediately, it became clear that it would not be smooth sailing.

Chapter 5
BOOTLEGGERS' PARADISE

Put yourself in the place of a hardworking Alaskan in early 1918 who likes to enjoy a glass of beer or a drink of whisky at the end of a long day of work. Your fellow citizens, over your objection, have just made one of the few pleasures you can both obtain and afford here on the edge of the frontier illegal. Are you going to obey the law or do whatever you need to do to get around it? It was a pretty obvious choice, at least for a large number of folks.

By the coming of prohibition to the territory in 1918, Alaskans had a long history of homebrewing and home distilling, dating back many years to well before the Klondike gold rush. As mentioned in chapter 1, legend has it that an army deserter taught the Tlingit how to produce their infamous hoochinoo or hootch, a sort of homemade rum. Northern home brewers, like home brewers everywhere, experimented with whatever ingredients were locally available. At various times they used barley, potatoes, Irish moss, champagne yeast, licorice, cinnamon, nutmeg, orange zest, hazelnuts, Epsom salts, honey, molasses and oatmeal in an attempt to produce something that was both alcoholic and tasty. However, at least for the stampeders, it seems taste must have been almost an afterthought. Here is how Tappan Adney describes one homebrewing process in *The Klondike Stampede* (1900):

> Whenever whiskey runs short the Yukoner falls back upon a villainous decoction made of sour dough, or dough and brown sugar, or sugar alone, and known as "hootchinoo" or "hootch." The still is made of coal-oil cans, the worms of pieces of India-rubber boot-tops cemented together.

ALASKA BEER

This crude still is heated over an ordinary Yukon stove. The liquor obtained is clear white, and is flavored with blueberries or dried peaches, to suit the taste. It must be very bad, for the manufacture is forbidden by law; they say it will drive a man crazy.

Any man desperate enough to make and consume the output of such a still was certainly not about to let a little thing like the Alaska Bone Dry Law stop him. In that respect, our hypothetical Alaskan had much in common with a significant portion of the population of the entire United States. While many, perhaps even most, Americans chose to obey Prohibition when it was imposed on them by the Eighteenth Amendment and implemented by the Volstead Act, a large minority did not. In fact, the Volstead Act pales in comparison to Alaska's Bone Dry Law. The Alaskan statute outlawed the very possession of alcohol, with a few tightly defined exceptions. The Volstead Act allowed individuals to continue to enjoy alcohol purchased prior to the start of national Prohibition, so the wine cellars of the wealthy were not threatened. Plus the Volstead Act included many more exceptions that the Bone Dry Law lacked, such as allowing farmers to legally have cider and other fruit juices that might happen to become alcoholic through natural fermentation. Initially, Alaska attempted to continue to enforce its stricter standards, but in October 1923, in the case of the *United States v. Boland*, District Judge Clegg ruled that the Volstead Act had superseded Alaska's Bone Dry Law.

Regardless of which law was in effect, the ways around it were too numerous to catalogue. Besides homebrewing, one could usually find a doctor willing to prescribe "medicinal" alcohol. Physician records from the period show page after page of patients suffering from the same malady ("debility") who received the same prescription ("Spiritus Frumenti" or fermented spirits). Walgreens had 9 stores in Chicago in 1916 and 20 in 1920; by 1930, there were 525 nationwide, all built primarily on the sale of medicinal alcohol. If one didn't want to go the medical route, why not become a rabbi? Kosher sacramental wine was needed for orthodox rituals, but since Judaism lacked the organized hierarchy of the Catholic Church, it had no mechanism to determine who was or was not a rabbi; hence the records of rabbis with names like Patrick Houlihan and James Maguire. Or you could always patronize a bootlegger.

The origin of the term "bootlegging" is slightly obscure, though the most likely explanation seems to be that it originated during the Civil War to describe how soldiers smuggled alcohol into dry army camps via flasks in

Dry Spell (1918 to 1976)

their boot tops. During Prohibition, it came to describe anyone smuggling or dealing in illegal alcohol on land, with the term rumrunning being used to describe sea-based smuggling. With its extensive seacoast and large land area, Alaska was home to many entrepreneurs of both flavors from 1918 until the end of Prohibition in 1933. Indeed, Alaska still has bootleggers today, as will be discussed in a later chapter.

Even before the Bone Dry Law, Alaska had its bootleggers and speakeasies. Anchorage was founded in 1915 as a company town for the Alaska Railroad; alcohol was illegal there even prior to 1918. But where there is an unmet need, commerce usually finds a way. A bootlegger named Paddy Marion kept a still in a small building across from the Alaska Railroad Station in Anchorage. The site was used as an Episcopal church, but the minister lived in Seward and only came to Anchorage to conduct services on occasion. During one of these long absences, a female parishioner noticed smoke coming from the church chimney and alerted the authorities, who found Marion busily tending his still. Since he was caught in the act, he was arrested and jailed, where he served as cook for the other prisoners. Still, even in jail he found a use for his skills, as he used the raisins intended for raisin bread to make raisin wine.

Another well-known Anchorage bootlegger was called Russian Jack. He was born Jacob Marunenko and was a Ukrainian immigrant who arrived in Anchorage in 1915, anglicizing his name to Jacob Marchin or just "Russian Jack." He operated a pool hall for a short time on Fourth Avenue, which likely doubled as an illegal bar. After it went out of business, Russian Jack became a fixture on Fourth Avenue in Anchorage, pushing a baby carriage up and down the street. Underneath the blankets in the carriage would be a container of illegal booze, from which he would happily sell drinks to passersby.

While Marion Paddy and Russian Jack may seem quaint and slightly comical, bootlegging was big business in Anchorage. A series of underground tunnels were constructed under Anchorage's business district so that bootleggers could make their deliveries and speakeasies could operate without being observed by the police or treasury agents. Even the home of Oscar Gill, local politician and eventually the mayor of Anchorage from 1932 to 1933 and 1934 to 1936, was later found to have been modified to support smuggling alcohol. Windowsills could be removed to send bottles up through the walls between the studs. Today the home is a historic bed-and-breakfast, where guests can still see pieces of broken bottles inside the walls.

As well as being lucrative and ubiquitous, the business of bootlegging could easily turn violent. On November 23, 1920, Anchorage was incorporated

Federal marshals with an illegal still captured in Juneau during Prohibition. *Alaska State Library P344-260, George Family Photograph Collection.*

as a first-class city; prior to that, law enforcement was the responsibility of United States marshals. On December 22, 1920, the city council appointed John J. Sturgus, an experienced lawman from Montana, to begin as chief of police on January 1, 1921, at a salary of $200 a month. Sturgus lasted just seven weeks. He was shot and killed with his own gun on February 20, 1921. Sturgus's murderer was never caught. The city council voted to offer a $1,000 reward, the mayor pledged an additional $250 and all other council members and the clerk pledged $100 each, bringing the total reward to $1,950. Sturgus's death was the Anchorage Police Department's first unsolved homicide and was always believed to be related to the smuggling of alcohol. The second chief of the Anchorage Police Department resigned after only a few months on the job, citing the overwhelming danger. The third chief of police, Harry C. Kavanaugh, lasted eight months in the office before being gunned down by a crazed drunk with a shotgun on January 3, 1924. Clearly, trying to enforce the law in Prohibition-era Anchorage was a dangerous job.

Dry Spell (1918 to 1976)

Other citizens around the territory had their own ways to circumvent the law. The town of McCarthy could only be reached by train from Cordova. When federal marshals were on the train, the engineers would add material to the train engine's firebox to change the color of its smoke, thus alerting everyone in town to hide or dispose of any alcohol. In Ketchikan, Creek Street was the place to go for a drink. In the mid-1920s, there were over twenty brothels on Creek Street; prostitution was Ketchikan's number one industry at the time. Brothels were frequented by men looking for a little company and some liquor, so rumrunners would smuggle in Canadian whiskey to supply the houses of prostitution and backroom saloons. Creek Street is built over the water, and the rumrunners would simply wait until a high tide at night and then would row their boats up under the street to deliver their goods under the cloak of darkness. Most of the structures on the street had hidden trapdoors in their floorboards to receive such deliveries. Skagway was a major transshipment point of goods from Vancouver in British Columbia to Whitehorse and Dawson in the Yukon Territory. Canadian liquor passing through the American territory on its way back to Canada was theoretically untouchable; in reality, more than enough "fell off the truck" to keep the thirst of the citizens of Skagway at bay. Every town in Alaska had its own methods; it quickly became clear that trying to keep alcohol from the hands of those who wanted it was a fool's errand.

While Alaska may have been awash in illegal alcohol, it was rare to find beer on offer. The same issues of logistics that confronted the bootleggers and rumrunners in the lower forty-eight also existed in Alaska—perhaps even more so, given the greater distances and smaller markets involved. Compared to distilled spirits or even wine, beer was bulky and perishable. It was much easier and more profitable to smuggle in a load of Canadian whiskey than to bring in kegs or bottles of beer. Like other Americans during Prohibition, many Alaskans lost their taste for beer and developed a taste for cocktails, which were originally created to disguise the awful taste of the rotgut spirits they were made with. Illegal breweries on a commercial scale could only exist in places like Al Capone's Chicago, which was large enough and corrupt enough to conceal them. In Prohibition-era Alaska, just as in most of the rest of the country, it simply made more economic sense to operate an illicit still and sell bottles of hootch than to brew and sell illegal beer. Beer in 1920s Alaska was something made to be consumed at home, with family and friends; hootch was what you made for sale.

By late 1932, with the nation in the grips of the Great Depression, it was at last clear to the majority of Americans that the Noble Experiment was an

ALASKA BEER

abject failure. In his excellent history *Last Call: The Rise and Fall of Prohibition*, Daniel Okrent sums it up well:

> In almost every respect imaginable, Prohibition was a failure. It encouraged criminality and institutionalized hypocrisy. It deprived the government of revenue, stripped the gears of the political system, and imposed profound limitations on individual rights. It fostered a culture of bribery, blackmail, and official corruption. It also maimed and murdered, its excesses apparent in deaths by poison, by the brutality of ill-trained, improperly supervised enforcement officers and by unfortunate proximity to mob gun battles. One could rightfully replace our prevailing images of Prohibition—flappers kicking up their heels in nightclubs, say, or lawmen swinging axes at impounded barrels of beer—with different visions: maybe the bloated bodies of the hijacked rumrunners washing up on the beaches at Martha's Vineyard, their eyes gouged out and their hands and faces scoured by acid. Or perhaps the crippled men of Wichita, their lives devastated by the nerve-destroying chemicals suspended in a thirty-five-cent bottle of Jake.[11]

Alaska and the rest of the United States had had enough. It was time for Repeal.

Chapter 6

REPEAL AND
RETRENCHMENT

B y the presidential election of 1932, the impetus behind the repeal of the
Eighteenth Amendment was undeniable. The Democratic candidate
for president, Franklin D. Roosevelt, was on record as favoring repeal, while
the unpopular incumbent, Herbert Hoover, carried the anti-alcohol banner.
After Roosevelt's inevitable landslide victory, the handwriting was on the wall
for the supporters of continued Prohibition. The Twenty-first Amendment
came up for a vote in Congress in February 1933. An attempt to filibuster
the amendment in the Senate collapsed after just over eight hours; it passed
by a final tally of 63–23. Two days later, the House debated it for a mere
forty minutes before passing it by a vote of 289–121 and sending it to the
states to be ratified, not by state legislatures, but by special conventions
called for that specific purpose. On December 5, at 3:31 p.m. local time,
Utah became the thirty-sixth state to ratify the repeal amendment, officially
ending Prohibition. Even before the ratification process was complete, the
president and Congress had found a workaround. On March 16, at the
president's urging, Congress passed a law declaring that beer of no more
that 3.2 percent alcohol by weight (or 4 percent alcohol by volume, as it
is measured today) was not intoxicating. Since the Eighteenth Amendment
had only outlawed "intoxicating liquors," such beer instantly became legal
to produce, sell and tax; the bill also reinstituted federal excise taxes on this
now legally nonintoxicating substance.

The Twenty-first Amendment restored the authority to regulate alcohol
to the states or, in Alaska's case, the territorial legislature. The second clause

of the amendment reads, "The transportation or importation into any State, Territory, or possession of the United States for delivery or use therein of intoxicating liquors, in violation of the laws thereof, is hereby prohibited." Some states chose to continue living with the crime and hypocrisy of Prohibition. The champion of this attitude was clearly Mississippi, which chose to remain legally dry until 1966, while at the same time levying a 10 percent state tax on illegal liquor sales. In 1916, Alaskans had voted overwhelmingly for the Bone Dry Law, an act even more restrictive than the Volstead Act, which imposed national Prohibition a few years later. What would they decide now? Happily, Alaska decided to return to a system of licensing. In 1934, the territorial legislature voted to establish a Board of Liquor Control, consisting of the territorial governor, the territorial treasurer, the territorial attorney general, the territorial auditor and the highway

U.S. Army soldiers celebrate with beer at the end of a training march near Fort Seward in Haines, Alaska. *Alaska State Library MS4-37-14-09, William J. Betts Manuscript Collection.*

Label from Pioneer Brewing Company's Midnight Sun Beer, brewed in Fairbanks. *Alaska State Library MS108-1-03, Labels Used on Alaska-Related Products Manuscript Collection.*

engineer. Alcoholic beverage regulations were adopted and subsequently approved by the U.S. Congress. Producers, distributors and retailers could again be licensed to ply their trade legally in the territory. Several breweries, perhaps motivated more by hope than good economic sense, tried to take advantage of the perceived opportunity.

In Fairbanks, at the time the largest city in the territory, two breweries went into business in 1934. The first, the Fairbanks Brewing Association Incorporated, was located at 103 First Avenue. It lasted only a year, going out of business in 1935. The second, the Pioneer Brewing Company, was located in Garden Island. This area north of the Chena River was once an island in the middle of the river, bounded on the north by a slough that has since dried up. Besides the brewery, it was home to market gardens and the railroad depot. The Pioneer Brewing Company operated until 1937, at which point it was taken over by its creditors, who continued to operate it until 1942, when it closed for good.

In Juneau, the territorial capital and second-largest city, a brewing license was issued to a G.E. Krause in 1933, but no beer was ever actually produced. Two years later, the Mt. Juno Brewing Company also obtained a license, but again, no beer was actually produced. These breweries all faced the

same competition from Outside breweries that had dogged their predecessors before Prohibition, not to mention the challenges of the Great Depression. Breweries in the western United States such as Olympia and Rainier were eager to ship their product to the Alaska market; with no existing brand loyalty, it was hard for the local Alaskan breweries to make a dent in their market share.

Oddly enough, the most successful brewery in Alaska during the post-Prohibition years was not located in the major towns of Fairbanks, Juneau or Anchorage, but in little Ketchikan. The Pilsener Brewing Company opened at 1651 Cliff Avenue in 1935 and operated—apparently quite profitably—until 1943. The ads for the Pilsener Brewing Company struck some themes that we have seen before and also some that would resonate with craft beer drinkers today. First, there was an emphasis on Alaskan images; names like Snowcap Pilsener and Alaska Lager made clear the local origin of these brews. The ads also

Newspaper ads for the Pilsener Brewing Company of Ketchikan. *Alaska State Library Advertisements-Alaskan-01 & -02, Alaska State Library Photograph Collection.*

focused on the quality of the ingredients used: "Pure Glacial Water," "Saaz hops," "No substitutes for malt—No Chemicals—Fully aged—Full strength." This was an interesting foreshadowing of how Fritz Maytag would present his Anchor Steam Beer some four decades later as "an old-fashioned beer, pure of heart." Finally, as we've seen in ads for earlier breweries, there was an explicit appeal to buy local and support Alaskan industry. It seems that the Pilsener Brewing Company of Ketchikan really was firing on all cylinders.

Unfortunately, even a small brewery that is doing everything right can find itself at the mercy of larger events. In the case of the two breweries still in business in Alaska at this time, that event was World War II. First with the attack on Pearl Harbor on December 7, 1941, and then even more so after the Japanese invasion of Kiska and Attu in the Aleutians in 1942, Alaska found itself on the front lines of the trans-Pacific war. Shipping to Alaska became difficult, dangerous and driven by military priority. Ingredients for brewing became more and more expensive and then finally impossible to obtain. In 1942, the struggling Pioneer Brewing Company in Fairbanks gave up; by 1943, even the formerly successful Pilsener Brewing Company in Ketchikan was forced to cease operations. Territorial prohibition in 1918 had halted commercial brewing in Alaska; now the exigencies of a global war ended it a second time.

That war, like Prohibition, did finally come to an end. However, unlike after Prohibition, no breweries attempted to open during the postwar years. Why not? With the military buildup during World War II, followed by the start of the Cold War, the drinking age population of Alaska had surged. Shouldn't this have represented a fertile market for a local brewery? Several factors pushed against the return of brewing to Alaska. First, the name of the game in the brewing industry at this time was consolidation; regional breweries were being purchased and closed by the industry giants at a rapid (and accelerating) rate. In 1946, there were 463 breweries in the United States; ten years later there were only 227, and by 1966 there were only 158. No one was opening new regional breweries anywhere; it was unthinkable. Another factor pushing against the return of brewing to Alaska was its improved link with the rest of the country. Thanks to wartime construction, the Alaska-Canada Highway now linked the territory to the lower forty-eight by road, plus new port facilities and airfields had been constructed; shipping goods to Alaska was cheaper than it had ever been. Beer imported to Alaska from big breweries on the West Coast had always represented the stiffest competition for local breweries, all the way back to the days of Robert Smith and his Skagway Brewing Company. Now this

ALASKA BEER

beer could reach Alaska quicker and cheaper than ever. Furthermore, the young soldiers and airmen who had come to Alaska during the war and stayed to make it their home brought with them loyalties to the brands of beer they knew from their homes in the lower forty-eight or their time in the service. With all these factors working against the idea of opening a local brewery in Alaska, it's no surprise that one did not materialize for over thirty long, dry years.

What *is* surprising is that when such a brewery finally did materialize in Alaska, it came from a place far, far away...

PART III
REBIRTH (1976 TO 2014)

Chapter 7
FALSE DAWN

In 1959, the citizens of Alaska realized a long cherished dream: statehood. The first Alaska statehood bill had been introduced in Congress by James Wickersham in 1916. Forty-three years later, Alaska was at last no longer an American colony, with its governor appointed by the president and its laws subject to approval or disapproval by Congress; it was finally a member of the Union on equal footing with the other states. One of the acts of the first Alaska state legislature was to create a three-member Alcoholic Beverage Control Board, appointed by the governor. State liquor laws were adopted based primarily on the former territorial laws. In 1970, the ABC Board was expanded to its current five members, with two being from within the alcohol industry and three being from the public. By 1978, there had been so many amendments to the alcoholic beverage statutes that they had become contradictory and unenforceable, forcing the legislature to embark on a complete rewrite. In 1979, when the new legislation was passed, provisions were included to allow communities to prohibit either the sale or both the sale and importation of alcoholic beverages. In 1986, the law was amended again to permit communities to go so far as to outlaw even the possession of alcoholic beverages, rather than just their importation and sale. Prohibition, as a local option, had returned to Alaska.

Several rural Alaska communities took advantage of the new local option, with some voting themselves "damp," meaning they outlawed the sale but not the possession of alcohol, while others went "dry," outlawing all possession as well as sale, with these prohibitions continuing to present day.

Indeed, in some remote communities, individuals can be and are arrested for simply possessing excessive amounts of such mundane foodstuffs as sugar and yeast, on the theory that they intend to use them to produce home-brewed alcohol. In 1995, Barrow, a city with over four thousand residents on the North Slope, became the largest town in the state to ban the possession of alcohol; currently seventy-seven communities ban both its sale and importation. Unsurprisingly to anyone familiar with the history of Prohibition, this ban on alcohol has led to thriving bootlegging operations to smuggle alcohol into these locales. Curt Wallace, a personal friend of the author, worked as the manager for North Road Liquors in Kenai during the early 1980s, shortly after the return of local prohibition in rural villages. He reports that the single most popular sale item in the store was cheap vodka in plastic bottles, sold by the case. This was the only product that the store stocked of which more was sold by the case than as single bottles, and it was one of the few in plastic containers. Since the plastic bottles were favored for air shipment due to their being both lightweight and unbreakable, Mr. Wallace always assumed the purchasers planned to bootleg the liquor into dry rural communities. In 2014, a bottle of cheap vodka that sells for $10 in Anchorage can be resold for $300 in a dry village; with profits like these, there is no shortage of Alaskans willing to follow in the footsteps of Marion Paddy and Russian Jack. Meanwhile, the Alaska state troopers continue to try to shovel back the tide and stem the flow of illegal alcohol, just like Elliot Ness and the treasury agents of old. To quote the immortal Mark Twain, "History doesn't repeat itself, but it does rhyme."

Speaking of history repeating itself, in 1974 there was another gold rush in Alaska. Or, to be more precise, there was a rush for black gold. The discovery of massive oil deposits on the North Slope necessitated the construction of the eight-hundred-mile-long Trans-Alaska Pipeline from the oil fields at Prudhoe Bay to the ice-free port of Valdez on Prince William Sound. To perform such a titanic feat of engineering, workers poured into Alaska from all over the world, creating a boom such as the state had never seen before nor has since. Before it was completed, some seventy thousand men and women had a hand in the pipeline project. Wages were excellent, with skilled tradesmen earning double what they could have made working in the lower forty-eight, plus free food and lodging. Overtime was the norm, especially during the long days of the Alaskan summer. During the winter, it really was the Klondike stampede all over again, right down to the isolation that gripped remote camps when the winter storms closed the roads and grounded the flights to Anchorage. Alcohol was one of the few distractions available, and the workers made the most of it. To this day, Alaskans still tell tales of the wild doings at bars, where pipeline workers blew their large paychecks on mad benders. The excesses of the pipeline boom era still cast a shadow over the state's liquor laws today. At that time, it was common for bars in Alaska to compete by offering happy hours with drink specials. Bars commonly offered two drinks for the price of one, and three or even four drinks for the price of one during happy hour was not unheard of. Naturally, these sorts of offers encouraged massive overconsumption and gave plenty of ammunition to the anti-alcohol forces. As a result, during the 1986 revision of the state liquor laws, all such special drink offers were outlawed. Even in present-day Alaska, any discount in the price of an alcoholic beverage must be in effect for at least one week and must be offered to all patrons equally. A ladies' night with cheaper drinks for women or a happy hour with drink specials, so very common in the lower forty-eight, are against the law on the Last Frontier.

The governor of Alaska during much of this period was the late Jay Hammond, a revered figure among Alaskans today. However, like most such revered leaders, Hammond excited considerable criticism and opposition when he was actually in government; reverence comes easier in retrospect. Hammond is most famous as the architect of the Alaska Permanent Fund Corporation, designed to convert some of the massive oil wealth the state had begun to receive after the pipeline became operational into long-term investments that would eventually generate revenue for the state. He recognized that North Slope oil was a non-renewable resource and worried that the day might come when it could no longer be counted on to fund the apparatus of state government. In 1976, he convinced the legislature and people of Alaska to amend the state constitution so that a minimum of 25 percent of future oil revenue would be used to fund an investment corporation, the idea being that when the oil finally ran out, the returns on this investment could support state government ad infinitum, hence the "Permanent" in its name. Hammond's true genius was also to structure the fund to pay annual dividends to each and every citizen of Alaska from its excess earnings, thus ensuring that any future politician who had the temerity to consider tapping the fund for his or her pet project would face instant and vociferous opposition from the public. Even today, almost forty years later, any suggestion to touch the fund's principal (valued at $51.68 billion in late 2014) remains the proverbial third rail of Alaskan politics.

Another of Governor Hammond's ideas was to build businesses in Alaska that could sustain themselves (and state revenues) during the ups and downs of oil prices on the world market. One of the ideas proposed was to establish a vibrant dairy and barley business in the subarctic, supplying residents with fresh beef and dairy produced in Alaska. A report, issued at Hammond's request by University of Alaska agricultural professors, supported the feasibility of the concept, allowing the governor to proclaim, "It is in fact possible that Alaska will be the prime agricultural state in the not so distant future."

To support this vision of a developing agricultural sector, the state started a lottery to sell off seventy thousand acres of land in the Interior, on which barley would be grown. Grain was planted, and the state bought nearly $1 million worth of railroad grain cars—twenty of them painted bright blue with the words, "Alaska Agriculture Serving Alaska and the World." Then it began building an $8.5 million grain terminal in Seward. Valdez, the town with the deep-water port and the terminus of the trans-Alaska oil pipeline, was envious. So it built an even bigger and better grain terminal that ended up costing the city upward of $30 million. There was vast optimism that Alaska would soon be producing bumper crops of barley. At this point, it occurred to someone in state government that you could do something with barley besides feeding it to dairy cows or shipping it to the lower forty-eight. Why not use it to brew beer in Alaska? The search was on to find someone willing to invest in a brewery in Alaska to turn what was expected to be mountains of barley into cans of beer to sell to those seventy thousand pipeline workers with paychecks burning holes in their pockets. After all, beer consumption statewide had gone up 16.2 percent even before the first section of the pipeline was buried in the ground. The *Anchorage Daily News* reported at the time that beer sales skyrocketed by 51 percent in Fairbanks, ground zero for the construction boom. With statistics like these, it did not take long for the state to find that willing investor, specifically the Radeberger Group from West Germany. Producers of such well-known brands as Radeberger Pilsner, Jever and Schöfferhofer Weizen, the Redeberger Group created a new subsidiary to build and operate a brewery in Alaska: Prinz Brau Alaska Inc.

By the mid-1970s, Anchorage had become far and away the largest city in Alaska, so there was no question that the new brewery should be located there. The state sweetened the deal by offering Prinz Brau a tax break of fifty-six cents per case for beer brewed in the plant being built in South Anchorage's Huffman Business Park. The brewery represented an $11.7 million dollar ($48.52 million in 2014 dollars) investment that employed forty locals, brewing lager beers made in accordance with the Reinheitsgebot, the German Purity Law. Two beers were eventually produced, Prinz Brau and Prinz Extra, and they were packaged in both bottles and cans. "Assessing the

Cans of Prinz Brau beer. *Courtesy of Elaine Howell Photography and Design.*

future, [Prinz Brau general manager Gerhard] Konitzky sees few clouds," the *Anchorage Daily News* wrote at the time. "Although it will take a few years to repay the investment, Alaska beer consumption has been jumping and will probably continue to increase." Unfortunately, Konitzhy's weather forecast turned out to be wrong, dead wrong. Prinz Brau was out of business by 1979.

What went wrong? As is usual in the case of spectacular failures such as Prinz Brau's, there were many factors that combined to bring about the disaster. First, the state's plan to grow barley was slow to get going; the first crop didn't even make it into the ground until 1978, by which point Prinz Brau was already struggling. It also turned out that the strain of barley used didn't grow particularly well in Alaska, due to the short summers. This was followed by a series of events right out of the Old Testament: a drought, a grasshopper infestation and, finally, roaming bison stomping through the fields. In the end, Alaska had invested $100 million in the project with nothing to show for it but empty railroad grain cars and useless grain terminals—so much for Hammond's vision of Alaska as a prime agricultural state. Still, while the lack of cheap and abundant locally grown barley was a

Alaska Beer

Rainier Brewing publicity shot of Alaskans drinking its beer at the foot of a glacier. *Alaska State Library P410-58, Framed Photograph Collection.*

disappointment, it shouldn't have scuttled Prinz Brau. After all, what about all those thirsty pipeline workers?

It turned out that most of those pipeline workers had been drinking some other brew somewhere else, long before coming north, and they wanted to drink "their" beer in Alaska, too. Beer companies from the lower forty-eight battled for a share in the small but thirsty Alaska market. Olympia Brewing went so far as to sign on as the major sponsor of the Iditarod Trail Sled Dog Race in 1984. As a new player on the scene, Prinz Brau had no brand loyalty to help it out. Plus the brewery immediately found itself embroiled in a labor dispute. With skilled workers in such high demand, the pipeline era was the high-water mark of union power in Alaska, and Prinz Brau was a non-union enterprise. The local labor leaders did everything in their power to oppose and undermine the brewery, including pickets and union-sponsored boycotts of its beer. As if its labor troubles were not enough, it seemed as though the company did everything it could to distance itself from Alaska and emphasize its Germanic roots. During its construction phase, the company held a public contest to choose the name for its flagship brand. Not surprisingly, the suggestions focused on Alaskan themes, with submissions like Grizzly Beer, King Salmon Beer, Mt. McKinley Beer and the like. After careful consideration, the managers of the brewery decided to call their flagship beer…Prinz Brau. By choosing to forego almost any connection to the state, the attitude they projected seemed to be that as Germans, they knew all there was to know about brewing beer and that Alaskans should be grateful that they had come here to impart their beer wisdom. While the labels did mention that the beer was brewed using "pure Alaska water," it seemed almost an afterthought.

Barley shortages, brand loyalties, labor troubles, culture clashes—they all played a part in Prinz Brau's singularly rapid demise. Still, the single most devastating misstep the company made was also the most simple: it sold a batch of bad beer to the public. Every brewer worth his salt knows the truth of the old saying, "You only get one chance to make a first impression." If the first experience a customer has with your beer is bad, it will very likely be a long, long time before he or she gives you a second chance, if ever. Oh, and they'll probably tell ten of their friends how lousy your beer was, too. At the time, many beer cans still had steel bodies with aluminum tops; use of the all-aluminum can of today was growing but was still not universal. In Prinz Brau's case, the initial consignment of cans they received in Anchorage had a defective lining, allowing iron from the steel bodies to leech into the beer. Iron in beer leads to harsh and unpleasant flavors. For a German lager such as those brewed by Prinz Brau, the maximum acceptable level of iron would be less than forty parts per million; the average level among such beers is less than twelve parts per million.[12] In comparison, some of the cans Prinz Brau put on the market tested in a laboratory at over two hundred parts per million of iron; one shudders to think just how bad it must have tasted. With such a series of missteps, Prinz Brau would have needed to produce a truly exceptional beer to overcome them. Unfortunately, what it sent to market (when it was not contaminated with iron) turned out to be little different than the beers from Olympia, Rainier and other breweries that were flooding into the state: just another bland and inoffensive lager, with little to offer in the way of flavor. So with nothing in the plus column to set it apart and lots in the minus column to hold it back, Prinz Brau limped along until 1979, when a longshoremen's strike in Seattle cut off its supplies of malted barley, forcing it to cease brewing completely. By the time the strike was settled and shipments could be resumed, the estimated cost to restart the brewery was in excess of $1 million. The investors at its German parent company declined to sink any more capital into what they now perceived as a very bad deal, so Prinz Brau closed its doors for good. The brewery equipment was eventually dismantled and shipped to the Philippines, the building that housed it was demolished and today the only thing to show it ever existed is the occasional forgotten six-pack of Prinz Brau cans discovered when cleaning out a garage, basement or attic in Alaska.

The impact of this fiasco on the mindset of investors in Alaska cannot be overstated. To them, it was obvious that if a German brewing company with over $11 million in capital behind it could not achieve success opening a brewery in Alaska, then no one could. The fact that such a seemingly sure thing as Prinz Brau could go belly up in just three years convinced the "smart" investors that you'd have to be crazy to start a brewery in Alaska. Fortunately for Alaska, there just happened to be two such crazy people available. Their names were Geoff and Marcy Larson.

Chapter 8
UNLIKELY CHAMPION

With the closure of Prinz Brau in 1979, things were looking pretty bleak in Alaska with respect to craft beer. However, just as things were looking their darkest on the Last Frontier, rays of light were appearing in the rest of the United States. In 1978, the number of breweries operating in the United States—eighty-nine—reached its lowest level since the end of Prohibition; from that nadir, the number would rise steadily for the next twenty-three years. Fritz Maytag had finally turned the corner on making Anchor Brewing in San Francisco profitable, and he had already brewed the beers that would resurrect three styles that are so common today: porter (Anchor Porter), barley wine (Old Foghorn) and the ubiquitous India Pale Ale (Liberty Ale). The John the Baptist of microbrewing, Jack McAuliffe, had opened his New Albion Brewing Company in Sonoma during the summer of 1977; while it would eventually close in November 1981, before doing so, this first-ever microbrewery would inspire a wave of craft brewing pioneers, including Ken Grossman, the founder of Sierra Nevada Brewing. Grossman visited New Albion in 1978 and established Sierra Nevada in 1979; he released its first beer, the famous Sierra Nevada Pale Ale, in March 1981. By 1984, there were some eighteen microbreweries in operation, mostly in the western states.

Other forces were also coming into alignment to support the development and growth of craft brewing. Thanks to the tireless efforts of Charlie Papazian, in October 1978, the brewing of beer at home was finally legalized at the federal level. For the first time since the end of Prohibition, when a typographical error legalized only homemade wine and not beer, Americans could legally make their own beer. While homebrewing had certainly been taking place, its quasi-illegality had kept it in the shadows, made obtaining quality ingredients difficult and stifled the exchange of information among its practitioners. Following legalization, the next logical step was organization; Papazian took that step in December 1978, when he created the American Homebrewers Association and its magazine, *Zymurgy*. Now that homebrewers had the means to communicate among one another, the good craft beers beginning to be produced had a ready-made market; plus this new fraternity of amateur brewers proved to be a fertile seedbed of potential future craft brewing entrepreneurs. Someone also needed to create a common language for their discussions of craft beer, a shared vocabulary to be used between the growing numbers of craft beer lovers. That role fell to the late, great British beer writer Michael Jackson, who almost single-handedly invented many of the common descriptive terms for craft beer that we bandy about today. Jackson published his first work, *The World Guide to Beer*, in 1977. It was eventually translated into ten languages and was the source of the modern theory of "styles" of beer. The beers that Jackson so eloquently described in it served as inspirations to many of the pioneer brewers and homebrewers of the early 1980s. Jackson's numerous subsequent works continued to develop the language of craft beer until his untimely death from Parkinson's in 2007. All the elements were now in place for the explosive growth of craft brewing in the United States as a whole, but what about here in Alaska?

Now onto the stage of our story step two unique individuals; they are just the sort of unlikely pioneers who have filled so many pages of Alaska's history. The first of these is Geoffrey Larson. He was born the son of a foreign services officer in Caracas, Venezuela, and spent much of his early life growing up in various cities of South America and Europe, wherever his father was stationed. He spent his summer vacations on a relative's farm in North Dakota, learning about harvesting and working the land; Larson has said that this experience helped prepare him for his future rugged, self-sufficient lifestyle in Alaska. Eventually, Larson attended the University of Maryland to study chemical engineering, and in 1979, he began homebrewing, which had just been legalized the previous year. That summer, he decided to hitchhike to Alaska, but he didn't make it. He ran out of money in Montana, so he was forced to take a job as a short-order cook at Glacier National Park. That was where he met Marcy Bradley. She was a blonde-haired native of Florida who had just graduated college with a degree in photojournalism but was currently working as an auditor for the park. As luck would have it, her schedule of working nights and Geoff's of working mornings lined up rather well, with both of them being free in the afternoon. They started as hiking buddies, but soon their relationship blossomed into much more. At the end of the summer, Geoff headed back to Maryland to finish his degree, while Marcy took another auditing job at a different national park, this time in Alaska.

With his degree finished, Larson headed to Alaska and back to Marcy. They ended up in Juneau, with him working for a local gold mine and her employed by the Alaska Department of Revenue. He continued with his brewing hobby, and they often daydreamed about starting a brewery. After all, breweries were beginning to open all across the country, but there were none in Alaska. The only unique beers available were imports that were typically well past their prime after the long, long transit around the globe and then north to Alaska. Why not give Alaskans a taste of truly fresh, flavorful beer like Geoff was homebrewing? It might have remained just a daydream if destiny had not taken a hand. In 1983, the mine Geoff was working at closed down, and in his words, "We took it as a sign to start a microbrewery of our own."[13]

With Marcy keeping her full-time job to support them, the couple spent the next two years researching and planning their brewery. Initially, they turned to magazines, like *Modern Brewery Age* and *Brewers Digest*. These pointed them toward the new microbreweries opening around the country. Since he had no prior experience with the nascent craft beer culture, Geoff attended the Great American Beer Festival (GABF) in 1984 to get a feel for what was being produced and to meet some of the brewers. Started in 1982, the GABF of this period was nothing like the massive event it is today. "There were only one hundred beers in the hall and I tried 'em all…the first night," Geoff recalled. "Second night, I narrowed the list down to ten and focused on them." It was also a wonderful opportunity to meet the key players in the growing craft beer movement. "I met Bert Grant, Paul Shipman, Bill Newman was there from Albany and Matthew Reich from Manhattan. It was small. You probably met everybody that attended. I came back with stars in my eyes, going, 'Wow, this is amazing!'"

During the same trip, Geoff also visited some of the breweries in operation at the time. "I went to Utica, New York and literally spent an entire day with F.X. Matt [Matt Brewing Co., brewer of the Saranac line of beers]. I took the tour, a beautiful tour with a tour guide in period dress through the old-time brewing industry. Then unbeknownst to me, F.X. Matt wrote to Fritz Maytag, so as I was actually heading to Alaska, I stopped off at Anchor. This was the day before Thanksgiving, and he took me around the brewery and talked about beer. I got inspired from these two people talking about this industry, and telling me, if you make beer, make the best you can because you reflect on all brewers." Maytag himself drove Geoff to the Greyhound depot to catch his bus for Seattle and the ferry back to Juneau.

While Geoff was busy meeting the inspirational leaders of the craft brewing movement, Marcy was beginning to immerse herself in the historical background of brewing in Alaska and, more specifically, Juneau. As we have seen in previous chapters, Alaska has a long and proud history of brewing, back to its earliest days as an American territory. In the early 1980s, there were still old-timers around Juneau who had memories of the pre-Prohibition breweries and the beers they had produced. As word of the planned brewery spread, residents would contact the couple to offer up boxes of memorabilia from the early days of brewing in Alaska. Marcy sorted through numerous such boxes, containing just about everything conceivable from the old breweries: trinkets, trash, invoices and old raw materials orders. One item in particular caught her eye: a mention of Saaz hops in a 1907 newspaper article, in which the reporter interviewed the brewer at Douglas City Brewing. In the article, the brewer described the challenges he faced in trying to brew a traditional German altbier, a warm-fermenting ale, in Juneau's not-so-warm climate. The brewer also discussed his difficulties in sourcing Saaz hops from Bohemia, now the Czech Republic but in 1907 a part of the Austro-Hungarian Empire. Due to his supply difficulties, the brewer used only enough hops to balance the beer, with the malt being the dominant flavor element. A local collector by the name of Nick Nichols also had quite a bit of information regarding Douglas City Brewing, including invoices and old raw materials orders. Combining the information from the article and the old records, Geoff was able to reconstruct the recipe, and he began making homebrew test batches, trying to perfect it.

Feeling that they finally had enough information, the couple began working on a business plan. It would be a challenge establishing a brewery in a city with no road connection to the outside world, where everything to produce the beer except water would have to be shipped in. They decided that, unlike most of the micros of the time, they would begin by bottling their beer and not sell kegs. In an interview in 2012, Geoff explained why:

> *The need to be constantly looking at how you do things made us wonder: here's the way other people do things, but it's not necessarily how we have to do things. For example, traditionally, you would sell kegged beers, then*

The Douglas City Brewery, near Juneau, circa 1907. *Alaska State Library P87-966, Winter & Pond Photograph Collection.*

sell bottles. Since this was Alaska, I could picture our kegs going up to the Bering Sea and becoming crab floats. Regrettably, we were faced with a one-way container situation if we wanted to get our beer up north, so we bottled for the first year. We didn't do any kegs.[14]

They decided to name their business the Chinook Alaskan Brewing Company, emphasizing its rootedness in Alaskan history and culture. With business plan in hand, it was time to find some financial backing; their best estimate was that they'd need about $500,000. Unfortunately for Geoff and Marcy, the early 1980s were the proverbial tough investment climate. The country as a whole was in a recession, the Alaskan oil boom of the 1970s had become an oil bust and money was tight everywhere. Furthermore, the recent failure of the Prinz Brau brewery in Anchorage loomed large over any proposal to open a brewery in Alaska. The couple found themselves being asked again and again why they thought they could succeed when a group of well-funded, professional German brewers had failed and failed miserably. In the end, no bank would touch the project, so they were forced to seek out private investors. It took almost thirteen months, but the couple managed to find eighty-eight Alaskans from all across the state who were willing to take the risk. Few of them were craft beer lovers; most were just interested in

Geoff and Marcy Larson in 1986, taking a break from building the Chinook Alaskan Brewing Company. *Courtesy of Alaskan Brewing Company.*

seeing a new and invigorating business open during the terrible economic climate. With start-up capital in hand, they could get started on making their dream a reality.

After two years of planning, things began to take shape in 1985. From a neighbor, the couple rented two thousand square feet in an unfinished warehouse at 5429 Shaune Drive in an industrial area of Juneau. They ordered a brand-new ten-barrel brewhouse from JV Northwest, a manufacturer in Canby, Oregon; over the next decades, that company would supply the equipment for numerous craft breweries. Since they had decided to bottle rather than keg, they purchased a secondhand bottling line. Geoff attended the Siebel Institute of Technology in Chicago to further develop his brewing skills. To get some experience brewing on a commercial scale, he also spent two weeks working at Millstream, a regional brewery in Amana, Iowa. Last, but hardly least, he and Marcy got married.

As anyone who has ever been involved in a brewery start-up knows, things never go to plan. Brewery locations have to be prepared, equipment is delayed, inspections have to be conducted and permits obtained. Chinook Alaskan Brewing Company was no exception. Complicating matters, no one had applied for a brewing license in Alaska in over forty years, with the exception of Prinz Brau. That application had been prepared by the parent company's legal department, shepherded through by its attorneys and backed by its supporters in state government. Geoff and Marcy had none of those assets, not to mention that they were proposing to open a brewery on a much smaller scale, so it's not surprising that their proposal

Original label for Chinook Alaskan Amber Ale. *Alaska State Library MS108-1-01, Labels Used on Alaska-Related Products Manuscript Collection.*

took longer to prepare and to be approved. However, with enough time and hard work, anything can be done. Eventually, the Larsons were the proud holders of brewing licenses from both the United States and Alaska; all told, it cost $310,000 to get the company off the ground. In December 1986, with the help of ten local volunteers, 253 cases of Chinook Alaskan Amber Ale rolled off their secondhand bottling line and out the door.

While finally getting their beer to market was a watershed moment, it hardly meant that their struggles were over. The logistical challenge of trying to move their beers to the larger markets in Alaska, like Anchorage and Fairbanks, was immense. Sending a case of beer from Juneau to Anchorage entailed loading it on a truck; putting the truck on a ferry for a four-hour trip to Haines, Alaska; followed by a 750-mile drive that crossed into and then back out of Canada. To put this into perspective, when the brewery opened, even the U.S. Postal Service did not send mail directly between Juneau and Anchorage; mail between Alaska's state capital and its largest city went via Seattle. So it's obvious that a small brewery was going to have a tough time managing to do what the U.S. Postal Service could not. In fact, it was not until a shipping company convinced the post office to begin overland mail shipments between Juneau and the rest of Alaska that the brewery could move its beer north on a reliable basis. The trucks often had extra room after taking on the northbound mail, and the shipper was looking for something profitable to fill it with; cases of craft beer from the brewery fit the bill nicely. After the first year, Geoff and Marcy decided they could begin to keg their beers; when it was time to sample the first keg, then governor of Alaska Steve Cowper came to the brewery to ceremonially tap it.

Like most start-up businesses, Chinook Alaskan Brewing was touch-and-go financially at times during the early years. Marcy related one such moment during an interview with the author in June 2014:

> *I was doing the brewery's books at the end of the week and realized we didn't have enough funds in our bank account to cover the payroll checks which had just been issued. More money would be coming in the following week, but right at that moment, we couldn't meet payroll. I knew I had to get more funds into the account before our employees went to cash their checks at the end of the day, but we just didn't have any to put in. In desperation, I took an armload of T-shirts with the brewery's logo on them, drove to downtown Juneau, and starting going door-to-door among the businesses. In about three hours, I managed to sell fourteen shirts at $15 each. Not easy, because no one bought two, and it was mostly the people we'd been selling our beer to who bought them. I took the money straight to the bank to deposit. That's how we made payroll that week.* [15]

As tough going as these early days were, the brewery received tremendous community support, both from consumers and from volunteers. Unlike Prinz Brau, the Larsons had discovered how to tap into a sense of "Alaskan-ness," a feeling of pride in the unique nature of life on the Last Frontier that binds Alaskans together. It's the emotion that Robert Smith of Skagway and Bruno Greif of Fort Wrangell were appealing to when they wrote ads calling on people to support home industry before Prohibition. It's the emotion that the little Pilsener Brewing Company of Ketchikan relied on during the 1930s. It's what the Redeberger Group, for all its brewing acumen, couldn't harness: the simple pride of living in a unique and beautiful place, a place like nowhere else on earth. It would still be years before "Made in Alaska" would be a logo on local products (including the caps on bottles of Alaskan beer), but the sentiment behind it was already growing.

With sales firming up inside Alaska, it was time to take the show on the road. Geoff had attended the Great American Beer Festival in 1984 as an aspiring brewer; in 1987, he and Marcy returned as full-fledged commercial brewers, offering their Chinook Alaskan Amber Ale to an audience outside the state for the first time. It should be remembered that their Amber Ale was a more malt-centered flagship beer than was typical for start-up breweries in the mid-1980s, especially on the West Coast, based as it was on that 1907 recipe from the Douglas City Brewing Company. Despite pushing the boundaries of what was expected at the time, their Amber Ale took home two awards, taking third place in the consumer preference poll (a sort of People's Choice Award that the GABF no longer conducts) and a gold medal in the professionally judged alt beer category. Not bad for a company that had been actually producing beer for

Chinook Alaskan employees and volunteers celebrating its 100th bottling day in 1988. *Courtesy of Alaskan Brewing Company.*

less than a year. Returning to the Great American Beer Festival in 1988, Chinook Alaskan Brewing was again crowned with the victor's laurels, with Chinook Alaskan Amber Ale earning both another gold medal in the alt category and being declared the "Best Beer in the Nation" in the consumer poll. In addition to the recognition for their Amber Ale, the Larsons earned a silver medal in the porter category with a brand-new beer: Chinook Porter.

Smoke flavor has a long, long history in beer; up until around 1700, most malt was kilned using some form of smoky fuel, like wood. Inevitably, the smoke emitted during the process would flavor the malt (and the subsequent beer) to a greater or lesser degree. It was only the development of purer fuels such as coke and, eventually, modern options like natural gas, steam or electric-heated kilns that allowed reliably smoke-free malt to be produced. Here's what Geoff had to say on the subject in a 2012 interview:

Back 200–300 years ago, everything was filled with smoke. When smoke was referred to, it was almost always in a negative way because there was no such thing as a smokeless environment: if you had heat, you had smoke. So there was never any reference to smoke in a positive way. If there wasn't any reference to smoke, it wasn't because the smoke wasn't there; it was just at a level that was acceptable.[16]

With the exception of a few rare survivors like the rauchbiers of Bamberg in Germany, smokiness in modern beer came to be perceived as a defect, resulting from either the use of inferior material or some other mistake on the brewer's part. Of course, what was true for the more "civilized" parts of the world did not necessarily hold true for frontier Alaska. Geoff again:

Most of the breweries at the turn of the century were brewing and malting companies. I'm sure they were forced to be innovative. You're at the end of the supply chain here in Alaska, you've got a booming work force—the miners are working six days a week, 10 hours a day. These same malt houses were invariably making some of the more powerful beers—porters and stouts. One particular brewery really talked about their porters. So in 1900 there were a lot of dark beers being made in Alaska. Here we are: we're in Alaska, there are dark beers, there are malting facilities, and the only hard wood around here is alder. This was a frontier town; everybody was using wood for cooking and for heat. If you walked down the streets of Juneau in 1907, what you smelled was smoke. In a town where smoke is everywhere, it's probably in the beer. It wasn't out of place.[17]

Just like their frontier forbearers, most modern Alaskans are familiar with smoke-flavored foods. A large portion of the population harvests our local salmon to subsist on, and they often smoke this fish to preserve it. Those who don't smoke fish themselves have plenty of opportunities to taste both homemade and commercially smoked varieties. In the time period we are discussing, just across the street from the Chinook Alaskan Brewing Company, was the Taku Smokeries, owned by Sandro Lane, a business that smoked salmon using local alder wood. Geoff recounts what it was like:

Across the street a friend of ours had a fish-smoking operation. We'd get together routinely on a Friday afternoon. He'd bring over some of the products he had, we'd have our beer, and we'd commiserate. There was a point when we thought, boy, it would be great to make a beer touching on the history of Alaska and the fact that to get these dark roasted malts, the old maltsters were having to really crank up the heat, invariably resulting in some smoke. And here we are finding smoke is a perfectly legitimate flavor in both beer and this fish. It was an interesting investigation: he knew smoke, and we knew beer and malt, so we collaborated in making part of our grain bill that would impart smoke character. With smoke, there's a real balance if it is to appeal. Cross that line, and it becomes objectionable. Too much of a good thing is a bad thing. But in subtle uses, it adds a dimension that is very, very enjoyable. [18]

The end result of this investigation was the Chinook Porter that took the silver medal in 1988. However, this beer did not stop there. Being savvy enough to recognize lightning when it strikes, Geoff and Marcy soon began to brew their porter on an annual basis and enter it each year in the Great American Beer Festival. Since its first medal in 1988, this beer, now known as Alaskan Smoked Porter, has been awarded medals at the GABF an unprecedented twenty-one times, more than any other beer in history, plus another thirty national or international beer awards. Every American-made smoked beer on the market today traces its genesis to a small brewery in Juneau, Alaska, with a fish smoker across the street. Geoff Larson's mastery of the smoked beer became so legendary that he was asked to write the book on it—literally. In 2000, he and co-author Ray Daniels wrote *Smoked Beers: History, Brewing Techniques, Recipes,* part of the Classic Beer Styles Series, published by Brewers Publications.

Going into 1989, things were really starting to look up for the Chinook Alaskan Brewing Company. In 1988, it had added its second year-round beer, Chinook Pale Ale. Sales were growing, its beers were winning medals and the future looked bright. Then came a bolt from the blue: the brewery received notice that a legal action had been filed against it by Chinook Wines, a winery located in the Yakima Valley of Washington State, alleging a trademark violation. The winery had gone into business in 1983 and claimed that Chinook Alaskan Brewing was an infringement on its name. Geoff and Marcy were faced with a tough decision: engage in a long and costly legal fight to defend their business name, with no guarantee of the outcome, or change the brewery's name, with all the costs in paperwork, marketing materials and loss of name recognition that that would entail. It wasn't an easy decision to make, but in the end the best option was clear. Chinook Alaskan Brewing became the Alaskan Brewing & Bottling Company, which it has remained to the present day. In retrospect, it's even possible that Chinook Wines did the brewery a favor; under its new name, it was even easier for it to be seen as the flagship brewery in the state. For many a visitor to Alaska, the products of the Alaskan Brewing Company would become synonymous with Alaskan beer.

Alaskan Brewing (as we must now call it) continued to expand its stable of brews. Over the course of the next few years, beers such as Alaskan Frontier Ale (an ESB-style) and Alaskan Stout joined its year-round portfolio, with additional seasonal offerings like Alaskan Summer Ale and Winter Ale joining its Alaskan Smoked Porter. Alaskan Winter Ale is another nod to the history of brewing on the Last Frontier, as one of its ingredients is spruce tips, just like the beer brewed by Captain Cook in Alaska some two centuries prior. In 1993, Alaskan Smoked Porter was changed slightly, with a small increase in its alcohol level and the start of bottle conditioning (leaving live yeast in the finished product). After this modification, the beer demonstrated an unexpected capacity for cellaring, as the long-term aging of beer is called. Geoff theorizes that the same compounds that impart the smoky flavor to the beer act to scavenge any oxygen molecules that might leak into the bottle, thereby preventing oxidation of the beer and lengthening its shelf life. Whatever the scientific reason, now Alaskan Smoked Porter had gained another reason for popularity among beer lovers across the nation, and they began to buy each annual vintage by the case to cellar for years.

During its first ten years of operation, Alaskan Brewing grew at a volume rate of about 35 percent a year. However, growth brings its own challenges, and in 1995, Alaskan Brewing faced a difficult choice. The company had reached the limits of what it could do with its original 10-barrel brewing system; to continue growing would require a major expansion. But to fund the expansion would require taking on a large amount of debt, just at a time when overall craft beer growth in the United States seemed that it might be faltering. To help make their decision, Geoff and Marcy consulted their employees. The unanimous response: "Go for it."[19] The decision made, Alaskan purchased a $1 million 100-barrel brew house, along with additional fermentation tanks, and warehouse space was tripled. The brewery also upgraded its keg system and bottling line the following year. The increased production capacity was needed to support a significant expansion of the distribution of its beers in the lower forty-eight. The brewery began receiving recognition outside the craft brewing world; in 1997, the Alaska State Chamber of Commerce named Alaskan the Bill Bivins Small Business of the Year, and two years later, the Small Business Administration named Geoff and Marcy its Small Business Persons of the Year. That same year,

Alaskan Brewing, which had produced 1,500 barrels in its first year of operation, was producing 69,847. In 2005, Alaska Airlines began serving Alaskan Brewing beers on all its flights. More expansions followed, and by 2012, output had more than doubled again, reaching 139,930 barrels; Alaskan Brewing ranked as the sixteenth-largest craft brewery in the nation that year. Its annual production represents approximately 75 percent of the beer produced in Alaska, with the other 25 percent being divided among the other twenty-three breweries in the state. In 2010, Alaskan Brewing opened a retail store in the historic Simpson Building in downtown Juneau. The state capital is a major port of call for cruise ships traveling up and down the Inside Passage, with the ships docking in the downtown area. While there are several tours available to carry tourists the six and a half miles from the waterfront to the brewery, the retail store provides easy accessibility for those lacking the time or physical stamina. Open year-round, unlike many summer tourist–focused businesses in Juneau, the retail shop also showcases products made by other Alaska companies.

Since its founding, Alaskan Brewing has always shown exceptional sensitivity to environmental and sustainability issues. The corporate culture that the Larsons created is infused with a respect for the uniqueness and beauty of the landscape in which the brewery exists. Following the expansion

Aerial view of Alaskan Brewing Company in 2003. *Courtesy of Alaskan Brewing Company.*

in the mid-1990s, one immediate issue that arose was the disposal of spent grain. For most breweries in the lower forty-eight, this is not a problem, as the grain is welcomed by farmers as animal feed. However, there aren't very many farmers in the Juneau area, and the few who exist couldn't begin to absorb the much larger amounts of spent grain being produced by the ten-fold increase in brewing capacity. Shipping the heavy, wet and unstable spent grain out of state was neither prudent nor economical. To solve this problem, Alaskan became the first craft brewery in the nation to install a grain drier solely to reduce the moisture content of its spent grain to below ten percent. Dry grain is lighter and costs the brewery less to dispose of, and it is shelf stable, allowing for ocean transport. Ultimately, the grain finds its way to Olympia, Washington, where a processor combines the now too-dry grain with liquid yeast from Alaskan Brewing and wet grain from other nearby breweries to create an appetizing mix for livestock feed

Another area where the brewery is an innovator is in the recycling of CO_2. While available very cheaply in the lower forty-eight, the cost of shipping cylinders of the gas to Alaska increased their price immensely. However, CO_2 is one of the byproducts of fermentation, so why not capture it for later reuse? In 1999, Alaskan Brewing became the first craft brewery to install a carbon dioxide recycling system. There would be other advantages, as Geoff related in 2012: "The most common source for bought CO_2 is burning fossil fuels. Our CO_2 comes from the grain that captured that CO_2 originally from the atmosphere. We have more control over our ingredients, since our CO_2 has no possibility of fossil fuel tainting. We've increased our CO_2 recovery by 400 percent over the past 13 years."[20]

The search for greater sustainability and less environmental impact continued with the installation of a mash press in 2008, making Alaskan Brewing the first American craft brewery to do so. This device replaces the traditional lauter tun in the brewing process and is much more prevalent overseas in places like Africa, where brewing water is scarce. To use a coffeemaker analogy, the typical lauter tun is like a drip coffeemaker, while the mash press is an espresso machine. The net result is more efficient extraction of sugar for brewing from the grain, using less water. Given its current size, Alaskan Brewing represents a significant load on both the water and sewer systems of Juneau; the company is always on the lookout for any steps it can take to minimize its impact on the community. As Geoff says, "We're very aware of our connectivity to the land, to our social fabric in Juneau."[21]

Alaskan Brewing's latest sustainability innovation was so unique that it made national headlines. In late 2012, the brewery began installing a true

To reduce water usage, a mash press has replaced the lauter tun at Alaskan Brewing. *Courtesy of Elaine Howell Photography and Design.*

technological marvel: a $1.8 million boiler that could be fired by dried, spent grain, the first of its kind in the world. Half of the energy from the furnace creates steam to heat the brew kettles, while the other half dries out the used spent grain, some of which is used for fuel. The rest of the dried, spent grain is still shipped south. Now, instead of paying $30 a ton to have all its dried grain shipped south to become animal feed, Alaskan can burn a portion of that grain to provide much of the energy required to operate the brewery itself. The brewery's estimate is that the new system will cut its fuel oil consumption by up to 70 percent and save $1.5 million in fuel costs over the next ten years. Eventually, the brewery hopes to burn all its spent grain, eliminating the need to ship anything south.[22]

Alaskan Brewing took two more giant steps forward in 2014. First, it began to can its beers. Many craft breweries across the nation and in Alaska have begun to can their products, attracted by the lighter weight, greater recyclability and the superior protection from light and oxidation offered by aluminum cans. Given the active, outdoor lifestyle of so many Alaskans, a light and unbreakable container is highly desirable; there's nothing like pieces of a broken bottle scattered all over the bottom of the boat to ruin a good fishing trip. For hikers, cans, which can be crushed when empty, are much

Geoff and Marcy Larson in June 2014. *Courtesy of Elaine Howell Photography and Design.*

easier to pack out than heavier glass bottles. Initially, Alaskan has limited the production of canned beers to two flagship brands, Alaskan Amber and its Freeride American Pale Ale, and is only distributing the cans in Alaska. The brewery was compelled to limit can production by a lack of space.

That's where the second giant step comes in. In April 2014, Alaskan began a two-phase expansion of its brewery. Phase one will allow for Alaskan to join its two existing buildings together in order to make more room for packaging and warehousing. It will also bring greater efficiency to operations, as forklifts will be used to move supplies and product instead of the current system of trucking beer between the two buildings. This phase should be finished by February 2015. The planned second phase will see the creation of new retail space to expand the brewery's gift shop and tasting room. Completion of phase one will allow the production of canned beers to be increased and distribution expanded into Alaskan Brewing's markets in the lower forty-eight.

Today, the Alaskan Brewing Company stands like a colossus over the craft brewing scene in Alaska. The little company that Geoff and Marcy Larson started some twenty-eight years ago has grown into one of the largest and most respected manufacturing businesses in the state. Alaskan's beers are distributed in Arizona, California, Colorado, Idaho, Michigan, Minnesota, Montana, Nevada, New Mexico, North Dakota, Oregon, South Dakota, Texas, Washington, Wisconsin and Wyoming. Its beers have brought home more than one hundred major medals and awards, almost half of which are gold, and the brewery has received a dozen awards as a business. Despite its phenomenal growth and tremendous economic successes, Alaskan Brewing has managed to sustain a strong commitment to both the local community and the natural environment in which it functions. All in all, it is a magnificent achievement and one that Geoff and Marcy Larson have every right to be proud of. However, the single greatest achievement of the Larsons and the company they founded is likely this: they showed it was possible to have a successful craft brewery on the Last Frontier. Like Lewis and Clark, they blazed a trail that others could follow. Not all the would-be craft brewers who came after them would be successful, any more than every pioneer who started across the prairie would make it to the Pacific; there's nothing guaranteed in this life, especially when it comes to starting a craft brewery. Still, Alaskan Brewing's spectacular success put an end to the prevailing belief that Prinz Brau's failure meant a successful brewery was impossible in this state. By the start of the 1990s, there were others willing to make the same leap of faith that Geoff and Marcy Larson took in 1986.

Chapter 9
THE BIG TOWN

By the early 1990s, craft brewing was really taking off around the country. In 1990, there were 284 breweries in the United States, a vast improvement from the paltry 89 in existence in 1978, and all the growth had been in craft breweries and brewpubs. One of that number was, of course, Alaskan Brewing Company in Juneau; but besides Alaskan there was as yet no other brewery anywhere in the state. The next logical place for a brewery to open in Alaska would be Anchorage, which was by this time far and away the largest city in the state. Beer is consumed by people, so it made sense to brew beer where there were the most people to drink it. The first brewery out of the gate in the spring of 1990 was the Yukon Brewing and Bottling Company. Not to be confused with the current-day Yukon Brewing Company, located in Whitehorse, the capital of Canada's Yukon Territory, this brewing company was headed up by H.A. "Buz" Hoffman, the former president of Alaska Continental Bank, who raised some $500,000 in capital via a private stock offering. The brewery was located on the corner of Seventy-First and Spring Streets and drew its water from an artesian well on the property. About $200,000 worth of equipment was purchased with an eye toward producing a beer named Arctic Gold Pilsner. Yukon's brewmaster was Adolf Zeman, who had worked in his father's brewery in his native Czechoslovakia and had first approached Hoffman with the idea of founding the brewery. The first cases of Arctic Gold hit store shelves in June and were well received; there was even talk of building a new brewery in a tourist-attraction theme park. However, disaster was just around the corner.

When Yukon Brewing and Bottling was being established, brewing equipment was in short supply on the Last Frontier. Rather than order in fermentation vessels from Outside, with all the shipping cost that entailed, the brewery hired local welders to fabricate square, open fermenters. Unfortunately, these welders had no experience constructing brewery equipment and were not aware of some of the potential pitfalls. In this instance, after welding the fermenters, they used grinders on the interior side of the welds, which lefts a myriad of small scratches on the surface. The scratches made the vessels almost impossible to properly sanitize once they had been put into service. Yukon Brewing was able to produce a couple excellent batches of its Arctic Gold Pilsner, but soon everything it produced was badly infected and almost undrinkable. With its reputation ruined with the consumer and lacking the capital to purchase properly constructed brewing equipment, Yukon Brewing and Bottling Company went bust in 1992.[23]

Now it's time to introduce another of those unique personalities who seem to pop up so frequently in the history of beer in Alaska: Ray Hodge. Hodge had traveled south in 1981 to take one of UC–Davis's earliest "How to Build a Brewery" classes and then brewed beer at Sierra Nevada, Redhook and the now defunct River City Brewery. He'd come back to Alaska planning to build his own brewery but had ended up running a honey and health food store in the unique town of Homer, on the Kenai Peninsula south of Anchorage. Homer was founded in 1896, originally as a port for coal mining, but by the middle of the century, its focus had shifted to commercial fishing. In the late 1960s and early '70s, Homer was discovered by the artistic community. Today it is much less of a fishing port (though plenty of fishing does still go on, both commercial and by tourists) and much more of an arts colony, a "Cosmic Hamlet by the Sea," as some call it. There are numerous art galleries and stores selling local crafts, both in the main business district along Pioneer Avenue and in the tourist area along the Homer Spit. Homer is also the jumping-off point for numerous tours and excursions, including trips to the world famous bear-viewing spot in Katmai National Park. Here Hodge formed one of Alaska's first homebrew clubs, Quality and Quaffability, or Q&Q; this club would have a great impact on future craft brewing in Alaska.

After a few years in Homer, Hodge tired of the honey business, so he sold his shop and moved back to Anchorage. Shortly thereafter, he was contacted by Ike Kelly; Kelly wanted to start a brewery in Anchorage, and a mutual friend had recommended he talk to Hodge based on his education at UC–Davis. After meeting Kelly and hearing what he planned, Hodge agreed to construct the brewery and serve as its brewer; Bird Creek

Brewery—financed by Kelly and built by Hodge—sold its first keg of beer just before Christmas in 1991. Kelly mortgaged his home to raise the $100,000 needed to start the brewery, which was named Bird Creek after the town of Bird Creek just south of Anchorage, the longtime home of Kelly and his family. It was located at 310-B East Seventy-sixth Avenue in Anchorage. Bird Creek's annual production was four hundred barrels in its first year and eight hundred in its second; it would eventually reach an annual production of five thousand barrels.

Bird Creek's first and best-selling beer was its Old 55 Pale Ale, so named because both Kelly and Hodge were born in 1955. Based on a recipe from *Brewing Quality Beers* by Byron Burch, Old 55 was brewed from dried malt extract and whole cone hops. It was packaged with live yeast in both half-barrel kegs and twelve-ounce bottles, the latter being initially bottled by hand using a six-head filler constructed by Hodge. The late British beer writer Michael Jackson visited Alaska during this time frame and declared Old 55 Pale Ale to be "the most classic example of an English Pale Ale being brewed in America." Old 55 Pale Ale would eventually take a silver medal at the World Beer Championships in Chicago. If Hodge knew how to brew them, then Kelly had a flair for marketing and promoting beers. He converted nearly half of the warehouse that housed the brewery into a small concert hall, complete with elevated stage and professional lighting and sound equipment. Weekly concerts introduced hundreds of Anchorage residents to Bird Creek's beers. After a couple successful years, Hodge and Kelly had a disagreement regarding the direction to take the brewery; Hodge felt that the brewery should begin brewing darker beers. He said, "Dark beers are the future of beer in Alaska," but Kelly felt otherwise, and so Hodge left Bird Creek. He was replaced by Bill Chadwick, who eventually managed to convince Kelly to add a porter to the lineup. However, Kelly suffered some serious financial reverses outside the brewing business, including the loss of his home to fire. Eventually he was forced to close down the brewery in 1998, at which point he sold all of Bird Creek's brand names and recipes to the Silver Gulch Brewing and Bottling Company (more on it later in this chapter). Old 55 Pale Ale continues to be brewed by Silver Gulch to this day.[24]

The craft brewing scene in Anchorage continued to show signs of growth, with beer from Pacific Northwest breweries and Alaskan Brewing appearing with greater and greater regularity. Craft beer availability took a quantum leap in 1994, when Humpy's Great Alaskan Alehouse opened at 610 West Sixth Avenue. The brainchild of Billy Opinsky, Humpy's offered forty-one beers on tap, making it the equal of any taphouse in Portland or Seattle. With a rotation so rapid that it printed a new beer menu daily and a heavy bias toward Alaskan and regional breweries, the opening of Humpy's signaled that the Anchorage craft beer culture had come of age. More beers from more breweries would now be needed to keep those taps supplied.

Following his departure from Bird Creek at the end of 1992, Ray Hodge returned to beekeeping and honey sales, first in Fairbanks and then in Hawaii, but he stayed plugged in to the brewing business in Alaska. In 1994, he was contacted by Mark Staples, who, along with Barb Miller and Chris Cimino, was hoping to launch another microbrewery in Anchorage. Once again a mutual friend had recommended Hodge to Staples; this time it was Shawn Wendling, who was then working at the Budweiser brewing plant in Fort Collins, Colorado. Given his prior experience building and operating Bird Creek, Wendling had told Staples that Hodge was the perfect hire for the new brewery. After listening to what Staples had to say, Hodge agreed to take the job; so it was farewell to beekeeping, hello again to brewing, this time at the new Midnight Sun Brewing Company. Once again, Hodge would be building a brewery from the ground up.

Midnight Sun's original location was 7329 Arctic Boulevard, less than a mile from Hodge's former workplace at Bird Creek; the brewery shared a small building with Knight's Taxidermy, a business featured on the reality television program *Mounted in Alaska*. After helping select the site, Hodge had to design the brewhouse layout, find and purchase the equipment and then install and test each piece. At that point, he was finally ready to begin brewing. Midnight Sun released its first beer, Wolf Spirit Sparkling Ale, in May 1995. Several others soon followed: Kodiak Brown Ale, Mammoth Extra Stout and Fireweed Honey Wheat Beer, among several other mainstream brews. There were occasional seasonals, like Double Shovel Dopplebock, Autumnfest Marzen and Humpback Jack Pumpkin Ale. By 1996, Midnight Sun was producing about one thousand barrels a year, but by then Ray Hodge had moved on to another brewing project, Railway Brewing (see below). Mark Staples initially assumed the duties as brewer and then hired Jimmy Butchard as head brewer. Together they developed some more challenging beers for the brewery's "Three-Barrel Line" of specialty beers, which were served only on draft at select outlets in Anchorage. Beers in the line included a rauchbock, an abbey ale and Snowshoe White Wit Beer, the first commercial witbier brewed in Alaska.

All was not smooth sailing for Midnight Sun, however. The brewery was in the red for a while, and at one point the owners actually tried to sell it. Other local Alaska breweries had started up as well, and competition was stiff, so there were no takers. Midnight Sun also had a very acrimonious breakup with its distributor at the time, Odom Corporation; afterward, there were rumors of a $100 bounty being paid by that distributor to Anchorage bars for each Midnight Sun beer they would remove their draft lineup. Still, the brewery and its owners soldiered on. They experimented with having some of its beers brewed under contract at various Outside breweries but were unhappy with the quality of the beer produced. Butchard departed as head brewer, to be replaced by Kevin Burton. In early 1998, Burton left; as his replacement, Midnight Sun promoted a young employee with almost no commercial brewing experience by the name of Gabe Fletcher. It may have been a move born of desperation, but in hindsight, it looks like pure genius. In the first three years of its existence, Midnight Sun had four different head brewers; Fletcher would serve as head brewer for the next twelve and a half years. The results of his efforts will be discussed in the next chapter.

One of the challenges faced by both Bird Creek and Midnight Sun was the sudden explosion of brewpubs. The concept of the brewpub—i.e., a bar that brewed its own beer to serve—is probably as old as brewing itself, though it had begun to fall out of favor with the growing industrialization of brewing during the 1700s. Yakima Brewing & Malting Co, also known as Grant's Brewery Pub, was opened by Bert Grant in Yakima, Washington, in 1982 and is regarded as the first brewpub in the United States since Prohibition. While brewpubs had become common in the lower forty-eight by the mid-1990s, they were still unknown in Alaska. Then in 1995, Ken Pajak, who had been chef at the North Slope Restaurant in the Anchorage suburb of Eagle River for twenty-two years, convinced his boss that he could brew beer that would sell. As the story goes, Pajak had received a homebrew kit as a gift from his wife four years earlier. He gave some of his beer to his boss to taste; after one sip, his boss was onboard. An unused dining room became the brewery, and two Grundy tanks were welded together to create a fermenter. Ike Kelly of Bird Creek provided some help, and by the summer of 1995, Regal Eagle Brewing was up and running. "We just went ahead and did it—Alaska style," says Pajak.[25] The first brew out of the three-barrel brewhouse was named Copper River Amber; Pajak usually brewed twice a month, which was sufficient to keep half a dozen unfiltered ales on tap and meet demand at the restaurant. Pajak also made the occasional lager, such as an Oktoberfest, and also produced an annual barley wine, which he cellared for a year before release. In 1996, Regal Eagle produced seventy barrels, and its Copper River Amber took a bronze medal at the World Beer Cup in Atlanta. Eventually, Regal Eagle's annual production would reach three hundred barrels, but by then Pajak had moved on. In 1999, he took over one of Anchorage's best regarded beer bars, Café Amsterdam. He was replaced as Regal Eagle's brewer by Ken Stephenson. The second Ken created some new styles and kept the brewery busy until he departed in July 2003. The third Ken, Ken Hood, served as brewer until December of that year, when Regal Eagle closed permanently. However, long before its eventual demise, Regal Eagle had inspired a slew of other brewpubs in Anchorage and beyond.

The first out of the gate was Cusack's Brewpub and Roaster, a sports-themed bar located in the Northern Lights Hotel in mid-town Anchorage. Focused more on local hockey fans than the summer tourist crowds, Cusack's opened in October 1995 with Laurence Livingston as its brewer. Typically, Livingston kept eight brews on tap, alongside a dozen or so guest beers from Alaskan Brewing and craft breweries from the Pacific Northwest. Brews created by Livingston included Seven Grain Ale, Coal Point Porter, Mooseknuckle Stout, MacGrouder's Scottish Ale and the exceptional Cascade Creek IPA (7.5 percent ABV, 70 IBUs). Despite the excellent brews on offer, Cusack's owner, Mike Cusack Jr., ran into financial problems in 2002, which led the city to remove his brewing license and foreclose. Still, Cusack's is remembered for its groundbreaking beers and for being the first brewpub within Anchorage city limits.[26]

Gary Klopfer had been an investment manager in Anchorage since about 1980 and a homebrewer. He was good friends with Mark Wilson, who had opened Alaska Mountain Top Spirits Co., the first licensed distillery in Alaskan history in November 1988. In 1995, shortly after Regal Eagle Brewing opened, the two dined together at the North Slope Restaurant. Over a couple of Pajak's ales, the pair decided that they would be interested in trying to start their own brewpub, preferably in downtown Anchorage. The partners began looking at vacant properties that might serve as a suitable location; they settled on an empty machinery store at 737 West Fifth Avenue, between G and H Streets, about two blocks from Humpy's Great Alaskan Alehouse. The space looked perfect, and the rental price was right; Klopfer and Wilson applied for a brewery license and a restaurant–eating place license at that location and began looking to recruit a brewer and staff. Others were also looking to get into the brewpub game: Railway Brewing and Moose's Tooth Brewing in Anchorage and the Dillo Brewery in Juneau were also in the planning stages, but Klopfer and Wilson looked to have an inside track. Then they hit a major roadblock.

Rebirth (1976 to 2014)

With everything moving ahead, the partners were ready to sign a lease on the property, but when they went to actually sign the lease, they were informed that the owner, Bob Acree, had changed his mind about leasing the property. Given that they had spent the better part of a year and considerable funds on the project, Wilson and Klopfer were understandably upset and brought suit against Acree on the legal basis of estoppel, which occurs when a party reasonably relies on the promise of another party and, because of the reliance, is injured or damaged. Meanwhile, Klopfer began looking for another location. As luck would have it, the local chapter of the Fraternal Order of Elks had a building at 717 West Third Avenue, two blocks north of the property the partners had planned to lease. Klopfer toured the Elks' building and thought it would work, though not as well as the facility they had originally planned on. After thinking things over, Klopfer called Wilson and told him, "All I want to do is make beer." They agreed not to spend any more time or money pursuing their lawsuit against Acree and to focus instead on opening a brewpub at the new location. They called their lawyer and told him to drop the lawsuit.[27] Shortly after the lawsuit was dropped, Acree and his partner, Chris Anderson, filed for their own brewing and restaurant licenses at the Fifth Avenue address. It would eventually open in 1996 as Glacier BrewHouse, while Klopfer and Wilson would open the Snow Goose Restaurant and Sleeping Lady Brewing Company in that same year.

This page and next: Exterior and interior of Glacier BrewHouse, Downtown Anchorage. *Courtesy of Elaine Howell Photography and Design.*

With so many brewpubs opening, brewing talent in Anchorage was obviously in some demand. Several of the local aspiring brewers had formed a sort of informal guild, under the name SPARG, which stood for the Society for the Preservation of All Real Grain brewers. Members included Ray Hodge, his friend Shawn Wendling (who was back in Alaska), Laurence Livingston and Mark Hartman. At one point, they decided to decide among themselves who would apply for what job, so as to not get in one another's way. Shawn Wendling was given first choice, as he was the senior brewer; he'd been brewing commercially since 1986, first in Dallas, then at the Carver Brewing Company in Durango, Colorado, and most recently as a brewing supervisor at Anheuser-Busch's facility in Fort Collins. He chose Glacier BrewHouse. Hodge, with his prior experience at Bird Creek and Midnight Sun, was the next senior; he chose Railway Brewing. Third choice went to Mark Hartman, who went to Snow Goose.

Klopfer and Wilson's Snow Goose Restaurant and Sleeping Lady Brewing Company takes its name from Mount Susitna, also known as the Sleeping Lady, which can be clearly seen across Cook Inlet from the Snow Goose's spectacular patio deck. By the summer of 1997, Hartman had four flagship brews constantly on tap, plus another four seasonal brews. In short order, it was obvious that both this venture and Glacier BrewHouse would be great commercial successes, popular both with local Alaskans and the huge

Exterior and interior of the Snow Goose Restaurant/Sleeping Lady Brewing Company. *Courtesy of Elaine Howell Photography and Design.*

numbers of tourists who visited downtown Anchorage during the summer. But what about the third downtown brewpub that opened in 1996, Railway Brewing Company?

Railway Brewing was located in the Alaska Railroad Depot at 421 West First Avenue and was opened by siblings Richard and Mary Sassara. Ray Hodge, now working at his third Anchorage brewery, was at the top of his game. To quote from a craft beer magazine of the time: "Hodge juggles an amazing seven different yeast strains to produce one of the broadest selections of beer styles you'll find at any brewpub."[28] Railway bottled four of its beers: Ironhorse Nut Brown Ale, Solstice Gold Ale, Steel Rail Chili Beer and Alaska's first dry-hopped beer, Railway IPA (6.3 percent ABV, 42 IBUs). Unfortunately, as with so many start-ups, the owners did not prove up to the task of managing a business; they were especially poor at employee relations. With cash flow problems, they never even managed to pay rent to the Alaska Railroad for the space in the depot, which inevitably led to Railway's closure and eviction in 1998. Hodge had departed well before that, unable to bear watching another brewery crash and burn.

Not all the breweries and brewpubs that opened during this period were in downtown Anchorage. There was a short-lived brewpub in Fairbanks, Raven's Ridge Brewing, founded by local Fairbanks homebrewer Hal Tippens; it operated intermittently from 1994 to 1996. The famous name of the Skagway Brewing Company was resurrected in a brewpub located in the Golden North Hotel of that historic city; it lasted from 1997 until 2002. The Dillo Brewery, located in the Armadillo Tex-Mex Restaurant in Juneau, was opened by T. Terry Harvey in 1998; it also lasted only a short time. However, one other brewpub that opened in the summer of 1996 was an immediate success and is still going strong today. Rod Hancock and Matt Jones opened the Moose's Tooth Pub and Pizzeria at 3300 Old Seward Boulevard and founded the Denali Brewing Company to supply it with beer. Hancock grew up in Portland, Oregon, and had studied computer science in college, while Jones was an Anchorage native who had just passed the Alaska bar; neither much fancied working for someone else, so they decided go into business for themselves, making draft beer and stone-baked pizzas with toppings ranging from the traditional pepperoni and sausage to more epicurean ingredients like artichoke hearts, eggplant, spinach and grilled salmon. Hancock had a passion for cooking, and Jones had mastered the art of making beer at home. Both had spent many nights enjoying good microbrews and designer pizzas at Portland pubs and believed Anchorage was ripe for the same combination. They spent a year planning the business, which was named after a climbing peak that rises out of the Great Gorge of the Ruth Glacier in the Alaska Range, and borrowed $130,000 from parents and friends to get started.

Interior of Broken Tooth Brewing's production brewery. *Courtesy of Elaine Howell Photography and Design.*

The Denali Brewing Company, which was the initial name for the brewery portion of the partners' venture, was cobbled together from dairy equipment once used by a microbrewery in Portland, Oregon. It was originally located in north Anchorage, near Ship Creek. Owner Jones started out as the brewer and soon had a dozen or so ales on tap at the pizzeria, including the very popular Fairweather IPA, brewed with lots of Cascade hop character, and the full-bodied Pipeline Stout. The combination of gourmet pizza and craft beer was an instant success with both locals and visitors to Anchorage, allowing the partners to pay back their start-up loan within the very first year. In fact, demand was so great that the makeshift brewing system was having a hard time keeping up; to remedy the situation, when Railway Brewing went bankrupt in 1998, the partners bought its brewing equipment, lock, stock and barrel. This allowed them to continue to expand production, which soon became too much for Jones to oversee personally, leading to the hire of Clarke Pelz, who would be the head brewer for many years. Having outgrown its initial location, the brewery moved to its current location at 2021 Spar Avenue, taking over a former ice cream plant. Hancock and Jones also changed the name of the brewery, first to Moose's Tooth Brewing and then in early 2012 to Broken Tooth Brewing Company, which is still its name today. Along the way, its beers have won two gold and six bronze medals at the Great American Beer Festival, as well as a silver and bronze at the World Beer Cup. The partners have also opened up two more venues that both sell Broken Tooth beers: the Bear Tooth Grill and the Bear Tooth Theatrepub. Today, the Moose's Tooth does more business than any other non-chain pizza company in the United States. As its brewpub license from the state limits it to an annual production of 15,000 barrels, of which only 1,200 can be distributed off-premises, Broken Tooth routinely hits its annual wholesale cap; this has become the limiting factor in its beer production. Not bad for a couple guys who just didn't want to join the corporate world.

At the same time that the various brewpub openings were rocking the beer scene in Anchorage, others were bringing the gospel of craft beer to more remote regions of the state. The first production brewery to open outside of Juneau and Anchorage was the Homer Brewing Company in the town of the same name on the Kenai Peninsula. In 1996, three people—Steve McCasland, Lasse Holmes and Karen Berger—decided to open Homer's first commercial brewery, which was also the first craft brewery on the Kenai Peninsula. On September 21, 1996, Homer Brewing opened its doors in a twenty-three- by twenty-nine-foot space, using a cobbled-together three-barrel brewhouse. Over the next five years, Homer Brewing grew to produce over one thousand barrels per year using this small system. Here is how Karen Berger tells the tale:

> Homer Brewing Company came to be from a combined vision of the desire to live in Homer, create an income and for the love of beer. The Q&Q (Quality and Quaffability) homebrew club here in Homer that spawned several of Alaska's present-day professional brewers was the basis of brewing education. The timing of the mid 90s was an era of Alaska craft brewery openings that set the foundation (and the bar) for Alaska's beer culture. We felt sure if there was a brewery in Homer, our efforts would be supported by the community. The "commercial brewer," in reality is 2 people and 2 distinct jobs at Homer Brewing Company. Karen is all things administrative and Steve is all things brewing. Together we are commercial brewers.

In February 2001, Homer Brewing purchased its current location as a permanent home for the brewery. In May 2005, it expanded its production capacity by installing its current six-barrel brewhouse. Homer Brewing still prides itself on offering "Fresh, Traditional Country Ales to go," with all of its beers being cask-conditioned and non-pasteurized, so the

Steve McCasland and Karen Berger, owners of Homer Brewing Company. *Courtesy of Elaine Howell Photography and Design.*

brewery is exclusively focused on growler sales and local taps. In this, it set the tone for several of the breweries that would follow it over the next decade. Given the difficulties of transport and distribution across such a large state with so many remote communities, some breweries in Alaska would choose to focus almost exclusively on their local market, rather than try to produce enough beer for wider distribution. Assuming the beer they produce is of good quality, such breweries found that they could be almost guaranteed enough local support to stay in business, just like Homer Brewing Company.

Exterior of Homer Brewing Company. *Courtesy of Elaine Howell Photography and Design.*

Another sign of the maturation of the craft beer culture in Alaska was the establishment of two annual beer festivals, which have continued to grow and expand to the present day. The oldest beer festival in Alaska takes place not in Anchorage or Juneau but in the small town of Haines, with a population of less than 1,500. The Great Alaska Craft Beer and Home Brew Festival was first held there in 1993 and has been repeated each year since. The festival is held on a Saturday afternoon in May and serves as a fundraiser for the Southeast Alaska State Fair, which also takes place in Haines. In recent years, a gourmet Brewers' Dinner is held the Friday night before the festival; its 250 seats routinely sell out, as does the festival itself. The next senior beer event in Alaska is the Great Alaska Beer and Barley Wine Festival, held each January in Anchorage. Founded in 1996 by Billy Opinsky, the owner of Humpy's Great Alaskan Alehouse, this event has grown into a major festival, with more than eight thousand attendees sampling beers from across the state and around the world over a two-day period; early attendees included such beer luminaries as Michael Jackson and Greg Noonan. With these two festivals showing the way, today there are dozens of different festivals held throughout the year and across the state.

Following the wave of brewpub openings in 1996, two new packaging breweries opened in late 1997 into early 1998, one in Anchorage and the

Silver Gulch Brewing and Bottling Company in Fox, Alaska. *Courtesy of Elaine Howell Photography and Design.*

other in the tiny town of Fox, just ten miles north of Fairbanks. The first was the Borealis Brewery, which was opened by S.J. Klein in August 1997 at 349 East Ship Creek Avenue, Anchorage. Klein offered several different beer styles, including an IPA, a pilsener, a bock and a nut brown ale. Borealis managed to reach an annual production of about 1,500 barrels by the start of 2001; unfortunately, that was only about a third of what it would have needed to produce to turn a profit. In May 2001, Klein decided to shut down the brewery in Anchorage and to have his beers contract brewed by Silver Gulch Brewing and Bottling Company. Unfortunately, even with reduced production costs, Klein was unable to show a profit, and the Borealis Brewery closed the following year.

The second brewery was the aforementioned Silver Gulch Brewing and Bottling Company, which opened in February 1998; it would eventually be much more successful than its doomed classmate, the Borealis Brewery. Silver Gulch grew out of the homebrewing hobby of owner/founder Glenn Brady, and it was and still is the northernmost brewery or brewpub in the United States. Silver Gulch has become one of the most successful breweries in Alaska, with its bottled beers being distributed statewide. In March 2007, Silver Gulch opened the restaurant and bar currently located with the brewery, in 2008, an outdoor beer garden was added and in 2012, it opened an outlet on Concourse C of the Anchorage International Airport. As mentioned above, when the Bird Creek Brewery went out of business in 1998, Brady purchased its recipes and beer names, keeping many of them in production at his new brewery. Bird Creek's illustrious Old 55 Pale Ale continues to be produced to this day. Many of Silver Gulch's other current beers started out as homebrew recipes from Brady's kitchen, subsequently modified by longtime head brewer Levi Hansen. Hansen left Silver Gulch in the summer of 2013 and was replaced by current head brewer Matt Austin. Given its remote location, it made sense that Silver Gulch would focus its efforts on bottling its beers for distribution around the state, rather than trying to build an exclusively local following, as some other breweries in Alaska have done. But that meant entering the extremely competitive wholesale market and going head-to-head with other distributing craft breweries, both within Alaska and from the lower forty-eight. Here's what Brady had to say about it in a 2001 news article: "It's unforgiving in the Alaska market. If you make one mistake, you might survive. If you make two or three, you probably won't." In the same article, Dawnell Smith, who at the time was the head brewer at Sleeping Lady Brewing, offered the following comment: "'The bottom line is that it's hard to make money with a microbrewery when you're wholesaling it. People go to the store and they're like, 'I'm not paying $8 for a six-pack.' Well, that's how much it costs to make it."[29]

At the close of the 1990s, the brewing picture in Alaska had begun to assume its modern shape. Many breweries and brew pubs had been opened. Some, like Alaskan Brewing, Moose's Tooth, Glacier BrewHouse and Snow Goose/Sleeping Lady had clearly been successful. Many, like Yukon Brewing, Bird Creek Brewery and Railway Brewing, had failed and closed. For some others, like Midnight Sun Brewing, the issue was still in doubt. But what was certainly not in doubt was that in less than ten years, Alaska had gone from having only a single craft brewery in the entire state to having a vibrant and dynamic craft beer culture. At the end of the twentieth century, the future of brewing in Alaska looked bright for the first time in over eight decades.

Chapter 10

RISING TIDE

By the close of the 1990s, brewing in Alaska had achieved critical mass. With the success of Alaskan Brewing and the several Anchorage brewpubs, craft breweries were finally ready to move beyond the largest cities into smaller towns, following the path blazed by Homer Brewing in 1996. And who better to assist in this process than the seemingly ever-involved Ray Hodge. After leaving the doomed Railway Brewing in 1997, Hodge had moved to Palmer in the Matanuska-Susitna Valley north of Anchorage and established a six-and-a-half-acre organic vegetable farm. Still, when contacted in 1999 by a group of investors looking to start up a brewpub in the nearby town of Wasilla, Hodge couldn't resist the siren's call of the beer business. He put his brewery construction expertise to work setting up the brewpub but did not stay on long as brewer, returning to his organic farming business. Laurence Livingston, formerly of Cusack's Brewpub, served as the brewer for a time, and the brewpub was quite successful, being the first of its kind in the Mat-Su Valley, which was growing rapidly. However, serious monetary disputes arose between its owners, including allegations of embezzlement and theft, which eventually led to Great Bear Brewing being closed in November 2009.

The husband-and-wife team of Paul Wheeler and Jeanne Kitayama also decided to throw their hat into the ring. On June 21, 1999, they opened the Haines Brewing Company in the small coastal town of the same name. When asked why he decided to become a commercial brewer, Wheeler said, "Like many others, I started out as a homebrewer, because there was no such

Paul Wheeler of Haines Brewing Company. *Courtesy of Elaine Howell Photography and Design.*

thing as a real beer when I arrived in Haines in the 1980's. By 1999 I saw the niche for locally-brewed beer, and so with the encouragement of friends we started the Haines Brewing Company."[30]

Initially, Wheeler started off with fermenters cobbled together from old dairy tanks obtained from the lower forty-eight, before upgrading to closed fermenters. His small three-barrel brewhouse is located in Dalton City on the Southeast Alaska State Fairgrounds. Dalton City was originally constructed as the set for Disney's 1991 movie production of Jack London's classic Klondike gold rush tale, *White Fang*. Following the completion of

Haines Brewing Company, located in Dalton City on the Southeast Alaska State Fairgrounds. *Courtesy of Elaine Howell Photography and Design.*

the movie, rather than demolishing the buildings, they were moved to the fairgrounds, and one of them now serves as the cramped but historically accurate home of Haines Brewing. Its beers are only sold in kegs or by growler at the brewery tap, and distribution beyond the town of Haines is practically nonexistent. Yet, thanks to the same type of local support that made Homer Brewing a success, even the purely local demand has grown to more than Wheeler can supply. In late 2014, Haines Brewing announced plans to move out of Dalton City and build a new 2,700-square-foot facility in downtown Haines, including an expansion to a seven-barrel brewhouse. All Haines' beers are unfiltered and unpasteurized, so they likely would not travel well, even if Wheeler were inclined to expand his distribution, which he is not. Instead, he has chosen to focus on supplying his local community with the best beer he can.

This same impulse to be the brewery for a particular community—and only that community—was the motivation behind the creation of one of

Ben Millstein of Kodiak Island Brewing Company.
Courtesy of Elaine Howell Photography and Design.

Alaska's most isolated breweries, Kodiak Island Brewing Company. It was established in 2003 by Ben Millstein, a carpenter by trade and another avid homebrewer. In the 1990s, Millstein had spent several years in Homer and was a member of the renowned Q&Q homebrew club; he was friends with Lasse Holmes, Steve McCasland and Karen Berger, who eventually founded Homer Brewing Company in 1996. Inspired by their example, he decided to open a brewery on Kodiak Island a few years later. His first location was a small space just across the street from the docks in Kodiak Harbor; however, in a repeat of the pattern of Homer and Haines, Millstein soon found himself unable to meet local demand and in need of an expansion. In August 2012,

Interior of Kodiak Island's taproom, decorated with salvaged fishing boat booms. *Courtesy of Elaine Howell Photography and Design.*

Kodiak Island completed a move from its small original location to a new and much larger home on Lower Mill Bay Road.

Given its remote location, Kodiak Island Brewing also brews beers aimed squarely at the local market. A favorite way for the islanders to take their beer home is via a Quoin Beer Pig. These refillable plastic mini-kegs hold two and a half gallons of beer and keep it fresh for weeks; Kodiak Island Brewing is the second-largest consumer of them in the country. The last eleven years have built up a great bond of trust between the brewery and the people of Kodiak, which now allows Millstein the freedom to brew the occasional "palate-expanding" experiment, but he maintains a laser-like focus on his island community, with zero interest in trying to send his beers to Anchorage or other large markets in the state. When asked to comment on the future of the craft brewing industry, Millstein had this to say: "I do know that as an industry segment, we're in a period of unprecedented and explosive growth. I think there's still a lot of room for small, local operations like ours; what I call the bakery model, or for brewpubs. I'm afraid we might see another 'shake out' like we saw in the late '90s of distributing breweries. There's only so much space on the liquor store shelves."[31]

If a brewery realizes it will be at a big disadvantage in competing for shelf-space in the highly competitive markets of the larger population centers, then it makes perfect sense for it to focus instead on being the most popular brewery in its immediate area. In one sense, this means a production brewery functions almost like a brewpub, with a large amount of its revenue coming not from selling on the wholesale market, where competition is heavy and margins are small, but from selling its beers directly to the public via its taproom and self-distributing its kegs to local bars and restaurants. By keeping costs down and eliminating the distributor from the equation, a craft brewery can turn a profit, even in small and isolated communities, such as Kodiak and Haines.

While Millstein's "bakery model" might work for him, it was not an option for a production brewery in Anchorage. In the last chapter we saw some of the challenges that beset Midnight Sun Brewing Company from its founding in 1995 to the spring of 1998, when it hired its fifth head brewer in three years, Gabe Fletcher. While he was young and inexperienced, Fletcher brought two things to Midnight Sun that it desperately needed: stability and vision. On the stability front, Fletcher would stay at Midnight Sun for over twelve years, and his steady hand at the brewing tiller would allow the brewery to find and develop a distinctive style. The vision he brought was of a brewery producing challenging beers that stretched the limits of what the local beer drinkers had previously been offered. Here's how James Roberts, beer critic for the *Anchorage Press* under the pen name Dr. Fermento, described the change at Midnight Sun: "Over time the brewery got bigger, but I think the brewery's real saving grace is that it got bolder. Somewhere along the line, instead of trying to fit in, the brewery decided to stand out. Midnight Sun was one of the first, if not the very first, local Alaska brewery to dabble in producing Belgian-style ales."[32]

By 2003, Midnight Sun was producing such Belgian-style masterpieces as the tripel Epulche-Culotte (translation: Panty Peeler) and the strong, dark La Maitresse du Moine (Monk's Mistress). Not only did the local fans applaud the new direction, but beer lovers living outside Alaska also began to take note, with bottles of Midnight Sun's beers quickly becoming hot items on beer trading websites. As popular as these new releases were, they could not hold a candle to the furor created by Midnight Sun's tenth anniversary beer, the infamous M. With its single-letter name, this beer commemorated both ten years of operation and the brewery's 1,000[th] brew. Only a single batch was produced, and at first there was little reaction in the wider beer community, but eventually word began to circulate that M was something truly extraordinary, with the beer garnering numerous perfect scores on beer-rating websites. Within a few months, single bottles were being exchanged for several times their original cost. Within a few years, prices skyrocketed as the number of bottles available in the market dwindled. The last time a bottle of M was listed for sale, the asking price was over $1,500. After M, everyone in the craft beer community had heard of Midnight Sun, the wild little brewery making insanely good beers on the Last Frontier. The Belgian beer train was only just getting underway, however.

On June 6, 2006 (also known as 6/6/6), Midnight Sun Brewing Company released Fallen Angel, a Belgian-style Strong Golden Ale inspired by the classic Duvel, produced by the Moortgat Brewery in Steenhuffel, Belgium. Fallen Angel was an immediate and unqualified success and served as the catalyst for the brewery's next idea: a series of brews released sequentially throughout 2007. It was decided that there would be seven of these brews, each named after one of the seven deadly sins, an inspired marketing choice. From the release of the first beer—a 200 IBU, 10.5 percent ABV triple IPA named Gluttony—it was clear that these would be no ordinary beers. The series was immensely popular, both within Alaska and with beer lovers Outside. Recognizing a good thing, Midnight Sun followed up with another series of beers in 2008, this one called "The Planets," with a beer named after each of those celestial bodies. In 2009, the series was the "Crew

ALASKA BEER

Exterior of Midnight Sun Brewing Company's new brewery. *Courtesy of Elaine Howell Photography and Design.*

Brews"; each employee of the brewery created a beer recipe and appeared on the label of the beer they designed. The last series year was 2010, with beers under the theme "Pop 10." After that year, Midnight Sun decided to give the series idea a rest, instead focusing on rereleasing the most popular brews from the various series, under the name "Alaska's Most Wanted."

By the end of 2008, it was clear that Midnight Sun had overcome its initial difficulties and become not just a successful but also a world-class brewery. It was time for it to move out of the cramped building it shared with a taxidermist. In May 2009, Midnight Sun Brewing Company moved into a brand-new facility, located at 8111 Dimond Hook Drive. Besides a significant expansion of the space available for the brewhouse and fermentation tanks, the new facility contained enough space for a true taproom/restaurant, located on the second floor in the rear of the building. This space is called The Loft, and it immediately became a very popular lunch and after-work destination for Anchorage beer lovers. With the move to the new location complete, Midnight Sun Brewing underwent another massive change, with the departure of longtime head brewer Gabe Fletcher in August 2010. Fletcher had decided to strike out on his own, with plans to open the Anchorage Brewing Company, which will be discussed later. In his twelve and a half years as head brewer, Fletcher had produced some of Midnight Sun's most renowned and sought after brews; he would leave very big shoes to fill. He was initially replaced by

122

The Loft Taproom/Restaurant at Midnight Sun Brewing. *Courtesy of Elaine Howell Photography and Design.*

Ben Johnson, who focused his energies on moving Midnight Sun into a whole new arena: canned beers.

By 2011, with the success of such pioneers as Oskar Blues Brewery in Colorado, it was clear that craft beer in cans was now a viable option. Even in Alaska, Sleeping Lady Brewing had already experimented years earlier with hand canning its Urban Wilderness Pale Ale, with limited success. Kenai River Brewing Company of Soldotna had released its first canned beer in March 2011. As discussed in chapter 8, canned craft beer makes a great deal of sense for Alaska, for several reasons. For the folks at Midnight Sun, it was clear that they could either embrace this trend or get left behind. So embrace it they did, with a new canning line producing three of their flagship beers: Snowshoe White Ale and Kodiak Brown Ale, both of which date from the earliest days of the brewery, along with Sockeye Red IPA, their flagship IPA created in 2003. Cans began to roll off the line in July 2011.

With the canning operation up and running, Ben Johnson decided to depart Midnight Sun for greener brewing pastures overseas; he was replaced

Lee Ellis, Midnight Sun's head brewer, shoveling out a mash tun. *Courtesy of Elaine Howell Photography and Design.*

by Jeremiah Boone, a longtime member of Midnight Sun's brewing staff. In October 2012, Boone also decided to move on, at which point he was replaced by current head brewer Lee Ellis. Here's how Ellis described his road to becoming Head Brewer at Midnight Sun:

> *My brewing career began in my hometown of Redmond, Washington in 2002. I was a recently un-employed ski instructor and a friend recommended that I go apply at Mac & Jack's Brewery. I happened to walk in while they were shorthanded and was hired that day. I had been of age for just over a month and was in the very early stages of discovering craft beer. I had never home brewed or possessed an interest in anything more than drinking beer. It turned out that my mechanical, organizational, physical abilities were ideally suited for working in a craft brewery. I started out washing kegs and filling kegs, became a Brewer, then a Packaging Manager and now Head Brewer. It's kind of ironic that so many people imagine brewing to be their dream job while I never had any intention of making brewing a career, yet here I am 11 years down the road and loving every minute of it. Except for when I have to be up at 4 am to brew.*[33]

With Ellis at the brewing helm and demand for its brews growing, Midnight Sun Brewing Company has become a major force on the beer scene in Alaska.

In 2006, within weeks of each other, two new production breweries opened on the Kenai Peninsula, about a three-hour drive south of Anchorage. Kenai River Brewing Company opened in Soldotna, not far from its namesake, which is one of the finest fishing destinations in the world. Kenai River Brewing owner/brewer Doug Hogue describes how it came about:

> *I was an avid homebrewer for about 10 years before pursuing a commercial career in brewing. After moving to Soldotna, Alaska, I became friends with one of my current business partners, Wendell, who was also a homebrewer. One evening, after consuming a few of our creations, we decided to check into opening a local brewery in town. We built our business plan over the following year, found a nice little Specific Mechanical 10hl system, and the rest is history.*[34]

As is typical for the first craft brewery in a given area, much of the initial challenge Kenai River faced was to develop the local palate for craft beer. In a clever marketing move, for the first few years of the brewery's existence, each beer took its name from a particular fishing spot along the Kenai River. This helped create an immediate affinity for the brews among locals, as they immediately grasped the significance of each name. Once again, community loyalty played a large part in the brewery's success. Soon kegs of its beers were being distributed by Specialty Imports to Anchorage and beyond. By the end of 2010, Kenai River Brewing was ready to take the next big step and begin canning its products. Canning began in March 2011 with six-packs of its flagship Skilak Scottish Ale produced on a two-head manual canner, but by early 2013, Kenai River had upgraded to an automated four-head unit and was offering two additional beers in cans, Sunken Isle IPA and Peninsula Brewer's Reserve. By late 2014, Kenai River had maxed out its current location and was actively looking to move into a bigger facility elsewhere in Soldotna.

The second brewery to open on the Kenai Peninsula in the spring of 2006 was Kassik's Kenai Brew Stop, located in the town of Nikiski, about a thirty-minute drive north of Soldotna. This brewery is the Kenai Peninsula's version of a traditional farmhouse brewery. Its story began with the gift of a homebrewing kit from Debbie Kassik to her husband, Frank, for Christmas. Frank rapidly became a proficient homebrewer, and then the couple began

Doug Hogue, owner/brewer of Kenai River Brewing Company. *Courtesy of Elaine Howell Photography and Design.*

to consider the possibility of opening a commercial brewery. First, they constructed a thirty-six- by fifty-foot shed next to their home, and then in May 2005, they purchased a used brewhouse. They remodeled the building to accommodate it, with the help of family and friends. On Memorial Day, they opened for business as Kassik's Kenai Brew Stop. Initially, Kassik's sold its beer in kegs and filled growlers at the brewery, just like Kenai River. In fact, the two breweries were often confused, which led to a name change: Kassik's Kenai Brew Stop became simply Kassik's Brewery. Before long, Kassik's was also achieving the same sort of success that Kenai River experienced, based on strong local support. It signed on with Odom Corporation for distribution and began to package its beers in twenty-two-ounce bottles, which can now be found on sale across Alaska and even in Washington State.

While production breweries were opening, the brewpub entrepreneurs were not sitting idle, either. With the sustained success of the Anchorage-based brewpubs, it was clear that similar operations should be viable elsewhere in the state. First off the mark was the Skagway Brewing Company. As referenced in chapter 9, a brewpub by this name had operated in the Golden North Hotel from 1997 until 2002. However, in 2007, Michael Healy, a South Dakota native and longtime Skagway resident, spotted an opportunity and bought the

Exterior of the current Skagway Brewing Company. *Courtesy of Elaine Howell Photography and Design.*

derelict brewing equipment. He moved the brewery to a brand-new building, located at Seventh and Broadway, not far from where the original Skagway Brewing Company was located in 1898. On July 4, 2007, the Skagway Brewing Company again fired up the brew tanks and opened its doors, welcoming both locals and the thousands of tourists from the huge cruise ships that visit Skagway daily during the summer.

While Michael Healy was resurrecting a venerable brewery name in Skagway, Zach Henry was breaking new ground constructing the first brewpub on the Kenai Peninsula, St. Elias Brewing Company. When he and his family returned to his boyhood home of Soldotna in 2006 after a sojourn in the lower forty-eight, it was Henry's intention to open a production brewery. He had acquired the necessary skills through both formal education and working at the Yazoo Brewing Company in Nashville, Tennessee. However, he soon learned that not one but two such breweries (Kenai River Brewing and Kassik's Brewery) were in the process of opening in the Kenai/ Soldotna area. Rather than go head-to-head with them as the newcomer, Henry decided to shift gears and open a brewpub. Being a hands-on sort of fellow, he and his father did much of the construction of the brewpub themselves, finally opening for business in May 2008, just in time for the busy summer tourist season. The brewpub is a true family affair, with Henry's sister, Jessie Henry Kolesar, overseeing the food service, while he focuses primarily on brewing.

Zach Henry, the owner/brewer of St. Elias Brewing Company. *Courtesy of Elaine Howell Photography and Design.*

Since St. Elias opened for business two years after the two other craft breweries in the Central Peninsula, it was able to build on the initial work those breweries had done in educating the local beer palate. It was also able to capitalize on the local demand for a pleasant place to enjoy good food and excellent beer. The depth of this demand became apparent in the fall and winter of 2008, after the always-busy tourist season concluded. Henry had planned to operate reduced hours during the winter, opening perhaps only three

Interior of St. Elias Brewing Company. *Courtesy of Elaine Howell Photography and Design.*

or four days a week, expecting a big fall-off in demand. Instead, St. Elias remained busy enough to stay open seven days a week, even during the depth of winter, thanks to the loyalty and enthusiasm of local residents.

In the summer of the following year, 2009, another brewery opened outside Anchorage. Denali Brewing Company was the realization of a dream shared by its two founders, Sassan Mossanen and Boe Barnett. Mossasen was a successful building contractor and enthusiastic homebrewer living in the mountain town of Talkeetna. Barnett was teaching English at the University of Alaska Fairbanks, writing and publishing poetry and homebrewing in the Goldstream Valley outside Fairbanks. The two future partners met over a keg of Barnett's homebrewed pilsner. Together, they decide to open a brewery in Talkeetna, about one hundred miles north of Anchorage. On July 11, 2009, the Denali Brewing Company opened in downtown Talkeetna. The brewery began with a ten-hectoliter (approximately eight-and-a-half-barrel) system in a small space adjacent to the Twister Creek Restaurant, of which Barnett and Mossasen were also part owners. The brewery rapidly developed a statewide reputation for excellence, and demand soon began to outgrow its relatively modest capacity.

In July 2011, Denali Brewing Company opened its much larger production brewery, located on the spur road leading from the Parks Highway into

Sassan Mossanen, one of the founders of Denali Brewing Company. *Courtesy of Elaine Howell Photography and Design.*

Talkeetna. One of the driving forces behind this expansion was Denali's decision to begin canning several of their most popular brews, joining a growing tide of craft brewers in the state who had chosen this form of packaging. Currently, Denali offers four different beers in cans: Twister Creek IPA, Chuli Stout, Single Engine Red and Mother Ale. The downtown brewery had a beer garden added to it, enabling patrons to enjoy their purchases outside. The opening of the production brewery allowed the original brewhouse to be used to produce batches of some of the more unique brews from Denali, while the larger facility supplied the demand for the flagship beers. However, in September 2014, founder Boe Barnett announced that he was leaving Denali Brewing Company and moving out of Alaska. When asked about his departure, Barnett said, "The reasons I left DBC have to do with wanting to spend more time with my family, as well as spend more time on my other creative pursuits. I was never able to achieve a sustainable work-family balance in such a fast growing business." Sassan Mossanen remains at the helm of the brewery.

In the spring of 2010, one of the founding fathers of craft brewing in Alaska was back. Ray Hodge, fresh from a sojourn at the Weeping Radish Farm Brewery of Jarvisburg, North Carolina, returned to the state. He was summoned back by Randall Martin, the owner/landlord of the block of buildings that housed the former Great Bear Brewing Company, which Hodge had helped open in 1999. After watching the brewery implode in 2009, Martin purchased its equipment from the bankruptcy court and then asked Hodge to come back to Alaska and restart it, while also training Martin's son Randy to take over as brewer. Hodge agreed, but when he got

Denali Brewing Company's beer garden in downtown Talkeetna. *Courtesy of Elaine Howell Photography and Design.*

Denali Brewing Company's production brewery outside Talkeetna. *Courtesy of Elaine Howell Photography and Design.*

to Wasilla, he found a real mess. "There was still beer in some of the tanks. I think it had been there probably a year and a half, and I don't think it was that good to begin with," he said of the nasty liquid he had to pour down the drain. However, after months of hard work in the brewery and squabbling with state and federal licensing agencies, beer was finally flowing again in early 2011 from the renamed Last Frontier Brewing Company. With Randy

Martin as its brewer, today Last Frontier produces kegs for distribution and twenty-two-ounce bottles for retail sales to customers, with a focus on the local Valley area. His work in Wasilla done, Hodge returned to North Carolina, where he is currently the brewmaster at Blowing Rock Brewing Company of Blowing Rock, North Carolina.

While Ray Hodge was working hard to resurrect the brewpub in Wasilla, Gabe Fletcher was busy launching his Anchorage Brewing Company. After leaving Midnight Sun Brewing in August 2010, Fletcher made two unusual decisions. First, rather than focus on the local beer market in Anchorage or even Alaska, he negotiated with the international importer/distributor Shelton Brothers to purchase and distribute the lion's share of his production across the country and even internationally. Fletcher's reputation in the beer world after his stint at Midnight Sun was such that they were happy to agree, even before he'd brewed his first batch. Second, rather than purchase

Gabe Fletcher, owner/brewer of Anchorage Brewing Company. *Courtesy of Elaine Howell Photography and Design.*

his own brewhouse, Fletcher rented time on the existing brewhouse at the Sleeping Lady Brewing Company from owner Gary Klopfer, as well as space in that brewery's basement to locate his fermenters, barrels and bottling line. To be clear, this was not contract brewing, as Fletcher did all the brewing himself; he simply rented time on the equipment.

These two decisions allowed Fletcher to focus his start-up capital on what would make his beers unique: huge wooden foudres for his primary fermentation, a forest of used wine and spirits barrels for secondary fermentation and a state-of-the-art Italian bottling line to fill his 750-milliliter corked and caged bottles. His amazing success over the last four years is testimony to the farsightedness of these two decisions. Every beer that Anchorage Brewing produces is fermented entirely in wood, with the primary fermentation taking place in the foudres and the secondary fermentation (if any) taking place in barrels, before being bottle conditioned for release. Almost every beer is dosed with *Brettanomyces*, reflecting Fletcher's fascination with that particular yeast strain. The Anchorage Brewing Company's motto is "Where brewing is an art and *Brettanomyces* is king." Fletcher's interests extend beyond just *Brettanomyces*, however. He has constructed a coolship (a Belgian-style fermentation vessel) and begun experimenting with spontaneously fermented beers. He has produced sour ales, using both *Pedioccocus* and *Lactobacillus* bacteria. He has partnered with the Danish gypsy brewer Mikeller to produce several beers.

Asked about how he became a brewer, Fletcher said:

> *I never set out to be a brewer, it just sort of fell in my lap. When I turned 21 I found myself going to the liquor store and always walking out with something new. I was fascinated with all of the different beers to choose from, and back then, it really wasn't much. I walked into this brew your own wine place one day and asked if they needed any help, and they did. I worked there for a bit just helping out anywhere I could. I received a call one day from Midnight Sun Brewing asking if I would like to come work for them. A person I used to work with at the wine place started working there and recommended me to the brewery. I went in for an interview and that day I was put on the bottling line. Within a year and a half I learned the basics of brewing, an opening for head brewer opened up and I took it, promising the owners that I could do the job. It was daunting at first, but I eventually got in my groove and really started pushing the envelope of brewing, always trying new techniques and looking at brewing from a different angle. I put in almost 13 years there and finally decided it was time to move on and create my own brewery and start making beer on my own terms. That is where Anchorage Brewing Company was born. Now I focus on the things I love about brewing, Barrels and Brettanomyces. No more production brewing, I wanted to slow things down and make people wait for my beer instead of working to meet the schedule of the masses.*[35]

Acting on this vision, Fletcher began releasing his wood-fermented, barrel-aged beers in corked 750-milliliter bottles, which received instant acclaim across the craft beer world. Thanks to his agreement with Shelton Brothers, Fletcher's beers were available worldwide, thus overcoming the logistical issue that kept so many great beers from Alaska unknown for so

Exterior of Baranof Island Brewing Company in Sitka. *Courtesy of Elaine Howell Photography and Design.*

Interior of Baranof Island Brewing Company. *Courtesy of Elaine Howell Photography and Design.*

long. The demand for his beers was instant, and by 2014, it could no longer be met by brewing in the downtime available on Sleeping Lady's equipment. Fletcher began construction on a brand-new, state-of-the-art brewery at Ninety-first Avenue and King Street in South Anchorage, scheduled to open in early 2015.

Also opening in 2010 was Baranof Island Brewing Company in Sitka, the home of the first brewery in Alaska. Opened by Rick and Suzan Armstrong, the brewery began with a tiny 0.5-barrel brewing system, but demand forced expansion, first to a 1.75-barrel system and then to its current 10-barrel system. After supplying its local market for the first couple years, the brewery was looking to expand by 2014. On February 11, it was announced that Baranof Island Brewing Company was being granted a $350,000 development loan by the mayor and City Assembly of Sitka. The loan was granted from the Southeast Alaska Economic Development Revolving Loan, also known as the Stevens Fund. It would allow the brewery to purchase new equipment, including a canning line. By the end of 2014, Baranof Island had signed on with the Odom Corporation to distribute its beers to the rest of the state and beyond.

The year 2011 saw continued expansion in the number of breweries in Alaska, with three additional ones opening for business. The first was 49th

Exterior of 49th State Brewing Company in Healy. *Courtesy of Elaine Howell Photography and Design.*

Tourists in front of a prop bus from the movie *Into the Wild*, located in front of 49th State Brewing. *Courtesy of Elaine Howell Photography and Design.*

State Brewing, located in the small community of Healy, just a few miles north of the entrance to Denali National Park. During the summer, the community is extremely busy, servicing the hordes of tourists who come to visit the park. During the winter, the park closes and the temperature dips to around -40 Fahrenheit, along with plenty of snow, so it's easy to see why the brewery (along with many other local businesses) goes into hibernation for the winter. Like Baranof Island, 49th State Brewing started with a tiny system, a mere one-third-barrel brewhouse. Just like at the Sitka brewery, surging demand has driven several expansions, the latest being in February 2014, when a fifteen-barrel, three-vessel system was installed. 49th State has even decided to make a virtue of the necessity of shutting down each fall. Just before closing for the winter, the brewers fill every fermenter with beer that could benefit from a long, cold lagering and then turn the heat down to just above freezing. Come spring, these beers are released as part of the brewery's Hibernation series and have proved to be extremely popular.

The second brewery to open in 2011 was the King Street Brewing Company at 7924 King Street in Anchorage; it was founded by Shane Kingry and Dana Walukiewicz. Here's how King Street came about, according to Kingry: "While I too had daydreamed of opening a brewery,

King Street Brewing founders Shane Kingry and Dana Walukiewicz. *Courtesy of Elaine Howell Photography and Design.*

the first time Dana suggested to me that we pursue this together, I just chuckled to myself and let it go. I did the same the next time he brought it up too. It was only when he suggested it a third time that I realized he was serious. We got busy planning King Street immediately, and things haven't slowed down since!"[36]

Exterior of King Street Brewing in Anchorage. *Courtesy of Elaine Howell Photography and Design.*

The partners signed a lease on the brewery's location and purchased a new 10-barrel brewhouse from Premier Stainless. With all the pieces finally in place, King Street opened for business in September. Kingry and Walukiewicz decided that their initial beer offerings would be interpretations of classic beer styles, adapted from their successful homebrew recipes. They even eschewed clever or catchy names, simply calling their first brews King Street Blonde and King Street Stout; the idea was to let the beers speak for themselves. And speak they did. The good people of Anchorage embraced King Street and its beers enthusiastically. "Our biggest surprise was the strength of the immediate positive response," said Walukiewicz. "We had thought we might need to purchase more tanks in a few years. Instead, we were looking to expand less than six months after opening." That expansion took the form of two additional 40-barrel conical fermenters that were added in the fall of 2012, increasing King Street's fermentation capacity from 60 to 140 barrels. In 2013, King Street also began canning its beer in limited amounts.

The third and last brewery to open in 2011 was Arkose Brewery in Palmer, another major community in the Matanuska-Susitna Valley, about an hour's drive north of Anchorage. Arkose Brewery opened on October 11, the brainchild of the husband-and-wife team of Stephen and June Gerteisen.

Stephen graduated from the UC–Davis Master Brewers Program, while June completed the Siebel Technology Institute Sensory Beer workshop and Beer Judging Certification program. He handles the duties of head brewer, while she serves as creative director, including producing their logo, marketing materials and all their visual designs. June also develops special events at the brewery such as "Beer Meets Chocolate" and "Beer Meets Canvas." Like many other brewers, Stephen began as an avid homebrewer. He said:

> *I became a commercial brewer, because I didn't have passion in my career in the medical field, but I was a passionate home brewer. I put two and two together and realized that brewing was my calling. I am fascinated with the science of brewing and with a biology degree under my belt and a year working in a brewery, June and I headed out on the Alcan to attend the 6 month long [sic] UC Davis Master Brewers program in California. On our drive back, we began planning our own brewery. Five years later our dream came to fruition in October 2011.*[37]

As the first production brewery in the Valley, Arkose Brewery was immediately well received and very popular in the local community. By 2014, it had been so successful that the Gerteisens needed to hire their first two employees, besides themselves.

Exterior of Arkose Brewery in Palmer. *Courtesy of Elaine Howell Photography and Design.*

Stephen and June Gerteisen, owners of Arkose Brewery. *Courtesy of Elaine Howell Photography and Design.*

If 2011 was a great year for brewery expansion, 2012 was almost as good, with two new businesses starting up. The first was the Seward Brewing Company, a brewpub located at 139 Fourth Avenue in the downtown part of the historic town of Seward. It is housed in a historic building dating from the 1940s that was originally a mercantile store with offices upstairs. Most recently, the 13,500-square-foot building served as the Seward Elks Lodge, before being purchased by local businessman Gene Minden and extensively renovated. Following the rebuild, the building boasts a bar on the main floor, along with the brewery and retail store, a restaurant upstairs with magnificent views of Resurrection Bay and the surrounding mountains and private meeting/dining rooms in the basement. Like 49th State Brewing Company, the Seward Brewing Company is strictly a seasonal operation, open only for the busy summer tourist season and closed for the winter. In early 2014, Gene Minden sold the Seward Brewing Company to Erik Slater and his wife, Hillary Bean. Slater had spent the prior decade as the executive chef at the Seward Windsong Lodge, while Bean was the bar manager at a local restaurant during the same period.

The second brewery to open in 2012, and the newest brewery in Alaska at the time of this writing, was HooDoo Brewing in Fairbanks. HooDoo Brewing was the creation of Bobby Wilken, who, along with four other family members, opened the first production brewery in Fairbanks since the closure of the Pioneer Brewing Company in 1942. Wilken worked for five years at Alaskan Brewing Company in Juneau, learning his craft, before striking out on his own. Here's how he described his road to founding HooDoo Brewing:

REBIRTH (1976 TO 2014)

Exterior of Seward Brewing Company. *Courtesy of Elaine Howell Photography and Design.*

When I walked into my first brewery in the late 1990s, I was awe struck [sic]. I remember asking with wide eyes how beer is actually made, and picking my jaw up off the floor when they finished their explanation—I was hooked. I started to absorb anything beer related. Books, magazines, breweries, and of course copious amounts of beer. The two main things I just loved about beer and breweries were the fascinating, age-old brewing process from grain to glass, and the wonderful social aspect of beer drinking with friends and family. There is nothing I enjoyed more than hanging out in breweries, so I did that any chance I could get. 10 years before HooDoo poured its first pint, I put myself (and my wife Jessica) on a mission to open our dream brewery in our hometown of Fairbanks someday. I homebrewed quite a bit, then eventually started working on a business plan. The project of opening a small brewery was daunting, so I eventually tabled the idea and went to brewing school in Chicago and Germany to learn as much as I could about the craft. I traveled around Europe and the U.S., making notes and talking to brewers about equipment, techniques, and ingredients. When I returned to Alaska I got my dream job as a brewer—and then eventually quality control—at industry pioneer Alaskan Brewing Company in Juneau where I got to experience the small brewery culture in all its glory. After four years with the great people at Alaskan, I came to a cross-road [sic] in my life. In the end, I decided to throw caution to the wind and venture back home to Fairbanks to start the small brewery I had been dreaming about for so many years. I quit the best job I had ever had, and dove in head first [sic]. *Two years later, on Halloween 2012, HooDoo Brewing Company opened its taproom doors.*[38]

HooDoo Brewing is following the same "brewery as bakery" model favored by Kodiak, Homer and Haines Brewing. Its focus is almost exclusively on direct sales to the public via the brewery taproom, with no plans to expand its very limited availability on draft in Fairbanks or to ever package its beers in bottles or cans. Instead, the brewery seeks to produce classic beer styles, using genuine ingredients and authentic techniques, solely for its hometown. The local craft beer lovers in Fairbanks have responded very positively to this approach, and the brewery's taproom has become one of the busiest venues in town.

While HooDoo Brewing may eschew distributing its beers beyond a small number of draft accounts in Fairbanks, the brewery does frequently participate in beer festivals around the state. Craft beer lovers all across Alaska know to keep an eye out for the HooDoo Mobile, a former German fire truck. They have learned that when it's around, great craft beer is close at hand.

Exterior of HooDoo Brewing Company in Fairbanks. *Courtesy of Elaine Howell Photography and Design.*

Right: Bobby Wilken, owner of HooDoo Brewing. *Courtesy of Elaine Howell Photography and Design.*

Below: HooDoo Brewing Company at the Kenai Peninsula Beer Festival in August 2014. *Courtesy of Elaine Howell Photography and Design.*

Alaska Beer

At the close of 2014, it seems that there has indeed been a rising tide beneath all of Alaska's craft breweries. In the last decade, no brewery or brewpub in the entire state has closed its doors, with the single exception of Great Bear Brewing, and even that brewery is back in operation under a new name. It's been a long and winding road, full of hardship and bumps, but it seems that brewing in Alaska is finally here to stay.

EPILOGUE

As successful as Alaska's brewers have been over the last decade, there is ample evidence that the golden age of brewing in this state may still be ahead. In early 2015, numerous new breweries are in various stages of planning across the state. Baleen Brewing hopes to bring brewing back to historic Ketchikan; somewhere the ghost of the Pilsener Brewing Company is smiling. Gakona Brewery & Supply Company hopes to bring fresh beer to its namesake town in the Interior, while Growler Bay Brewing is working to bring local beer back to Valdez. Resolution Brewing Company in Anchorage will likely be open by the time you read these words, while Clarke Pelz's Cynosure Brewing Company is not far behind it. In the Mat-Su Valley, Bleeding Heart Brewery just completed a successful Kickstarter campaign to facilitate its opening in Palmer, while the indefatigable Ray Hodge is assisting in the planning of yet another brewpub for Wasilla, Bearpaw River Brewing Company. There will likely be others that have not yet been made public. Will all of them be as successful as the breweries that have opened in the last decade? Perhaps not, but the market for good beer, both in Alaska and Outside, does not seem to be at all saturated.

According to the Brewers Association, slightly more than half the craft breweries and brewpubs that open in the United States are successful.[39] When viewed against that statistic, it may seem that the twenty-four breweries and brewpubs operating in Alaska have been incredibly lucky. But when we look back at the amazing history of brewing in Alaska, this should come as no surprise. The risk-takers who climbed the Chilkoot Pass or panned the beaches of Nome didn't worry too much about the odds against their success, and neither did the men who brewed beer for them in Skagway, Nome and all the other frontier settlements. They just decided what they wanted to do and then went ahead and did it. That can-do pioneer spirit is still alive and well among Alaska's modern brewers. In the words of Ken Pajak, "We just went ahead and did it—Alaska style."[40]

Notes

Chapter 1

1. Bancroft, *History of Alaska*, 97, 130.
2. Ibid., 541–42. For a more complete discussion of this treaty, see J.C. Hildt, *Early Diplomatic Negotiations of the United States and Russia* (Baltimore, MD: Johns Hopkins Press, 1906), 157.
3. Borneman, *Saga of a Bold Land*, 106–9.
4. Van Wieren, *American Breweries II*, 12.

Chapter 2

5. Berton, *Klondike Fever*, 100.
6. Haigh, *King Con*, 11.
7. Adney, *Klondike Stampede*, 54.

Chapter 3

8. Borneman, *Saga of a Bold Land*, 207.
9. Ibid., 208.

Notes

Chapter 4

10. Spude, *Mascot Saloon*, 75.

Chapter 5

11. Daniel Okrent, *Last Call: The Rise and Fall of Prohibition* (New York: Scribner, 2010), 373.

Chapter 7

12. J.S. Hough, D.E. Briggs, R. Stevens and T.W. Young, *Malting and Brewing Science* (New York: Chapman and Hall, 1982), 2:779.

Chapter 8

13. Geoff Larson, "Alaskan Brewing Company," www.craftbeer.com.
14. Johnson, "Pull Up a Stool."
15. Author interview with Geoff and Marcy Larson, June 2014.
16. Johnson, "Pull Up a Stool."
17. Ibid.
18. Ibid.
19. McAllister, "Keeping a Head."
20. Johnson, "Pull Up a Stool."
21. Ibid.
22. Dunham, "Alaskan Brewing's Grain-burning Furnace."

Chapter 9

23. Author interview with Ray Hodge, December 13, 2014.
24. Wright, "Bush Beer," *BarleyCorn* (June/July 1998): 6–8.
25. Ibid.
26. Schell, Sarana. "Fate of Hotel Up in the Air."
27. Author's interview, December 2014.

NOTES

28. Wright, "Bush Beer." *BarleyCorn* (June/July 1998): 8.
29. *Peninsula Clarion*, "Borealis Brewery Gets Out of Production Business," July 16, 2001.

CHAPTER 10

30. Author e-mail interview with Paul Wheeler, November 4, 2014.
31. Howell, *Beer on the Last Frontier*, 1:55.
32. Roberts, "Celebration of the Midnight Sun."
33. Howell, *Beer on the Last Frontier*, 2:66.
34. Ibid., 1:28.
35. Ibid., 2:22.
36. Ibid., 2:50.
37. Ibid., 2:91–92.
38. Ibid., 2:133–34.

EPILOGUE

39. Cizmar, "Flameout: Breweries Come and Go." *Beeradvocate* (December 2014): 54.
40. Wright, "Bush Beer." *BarleyCorn* (June/July 1998): 6–8.

BIBLIOGRAPHY

BOOKS

Acitelli, Tom. *The Audacity of Hops: The History of America's Craft Beer Revolution*. Chicago: Chicago Review Press, Inc., 2013.

Adney, Tappan. *The Klondike Stampede*. Seattle: University of Washington Press, 1995.

Andersen, Thayne I. *Alaska Hooch: The History of Alcohol in Early Alaska*. Fairbanks, AK: Hoo Che Noo Publishing, 1988.

Bancroft, H.H. *History of Alaska: 1730–1875*. New York: Antiquarian Press, 1961.

Berton, Pierre. *The Klondike Fever*. New York: Alfred A. Knopf, 1958.

Borneman, W.R. *Alaska: Saga of a Bold Land*. New York: HarperCollins, 2003.

Chandonnet, Ann. *Gold Rush Grub: From Turpentine Stew to Hoochinoo*. Fairbanks: University of Alaska Press, 2005.

Daniels, Ray, and Geoffrey Larson. *Smoked Beers: History, Brewing Techniques, Recipes*. Boulder, CO: Brewers Publications, 2000.

Haigh, Jane G. *King Con: The Story of Soapy Smith*. Whitehorse, YT: Friday 501, 2006.

Hindy, Steve. *The Craft Beer Revolution: How a Band of Microbrewers Is Transforming the World's Favorite Drink*. New York: St. Martin's Press, 2014.

Howell, Bill. *Beer on the Last Frontier: The Craft Breweries of Alaska*. Vol. 1. *Kenai Peninsula and Kodiak Island Breweries*. N.p.: self-published, 2012.

———. *Beer on the Last Frontier: The Craft Breweries of Alaska*. Vol. 2. *Anchorage, Fairbanks, and Everything In Between*. N.p.: self-published, 2013.

Bibliography

Kania, Leon W. *The Alaskan Bootlegger's Bible*. Wasilla, AK: Happy Mountain Publications, 2000.

Spude, Catherine H. *The Mascot Saloon: Archaeological Investigations in Skagway, Alaska*. Vol. 10. Anchorage, AK: National Park Service, 2006.

Van Wieren, D.P. *American Breweries II*. West Point, PA: Eastern Coast Breweriana Association, 1995.

Articles

Anderson, Ben. "What's in a Name? Moose's Tooth Rebrands Brewery." *Anchorage Daily News*, February 5, 2012.

Cizmar, Martin. "Flameout: Breweries Come and Go, Even in a Growing Market." *Beeradvocate* (December 2014).

D'Oro, Rachel. "Moose's Tooth." *Anchorage Daily News*, December 14, 1998.

Dunham, Mike. "Alaskan Brewing's Grain-burning Furnace is the First in the World." *Anchorage Daily News*, January 18, 2013.

Johnson, Julie. "Pull Up a Stool with Geoff and Marcy Larson." *All About Beer* (March 2012): 12.

Marquis, Kim. "Alaskan Brewing Expands to Downtown." *Juneau Empire*, February 10, 2010.

McAllister, Bill. "Keeping a Head: Local Couple Expanding Brewery at a Consistent, Careful Pace," *Juneau Empire*, March 14, 2000.

Medred, Craig. "Dreaming Big: Six Alaskan Boondoggles." *Alaska Dispatch*, October 10, 2011.

Musgrove, Michael. "Brewing Beer Alaska Style." *Alaska Business Monthly* (July 1993): 36–38.

Nelson, Courtney. "The Art of Brewing Beer." *Juneau Empire*, May 25, 2011.

Pohl-Smith, Jeanine. "Dillo Brewery: Small But It's Popular." *Juneau Empire*, July 20, 1999.

Roberts, James. "Celebration of the Midnight Sun." *Anchorage Press*, May 8, 2014.

———. "Eagle River Brewery Now Mines a Mother Lode." *Anchorage Press*, April 22, 2004.

———. "Precious Beers on the Horizon." *Anchorage Press*, October 13, 2010.

Schell, Sarana. "The Fate of Hotel That Helped Pioneer Color Television and Brewpubs Is Up in the Air, Again." *Anchorage Daily News*, April 1, 2005.

Wright, DeWayne. "Bush Beer: Craftbrewing in the Last Frontier." *BarleyCorn* (June/July 1998).

Bibliography

Interviews

Many interviews were conducted in person or via phone and were recorded. The recordings and transcripts of these and other interviews, as well as e-mail correspondence, are in the possession of the author.

Gurcke, Karl. In-person interview, May 21, 2014.
Hodge, Ray. Phone interview, December 13, 2014.
Klopfer, Gary. Phone interview, December 3, 2014.
Larson, Geoffrey and Marcy. In-person interview, June 18, 2014.
Millstein, Ben. In-person interview, August 16, 2012.
Wallace, Curtis. In-person interview, September 5, 2014.
Wheeler, Paul. E-mail interview, November 4, 2014.

Unpublished Materials

Corrington, Dennis, and Nancy Corrington. "Skagway's Gold Rush Breweries, 1897–1906." Unpublished paper. Golden North Hotel, Skagway, n.d.
Sparks, Larry Arthur. "The Failure of Prohibition in Alaska: 1884 to 1900." Master's thesis, Western Washington State College, 1974.

INDEX

Index

Index

Index

About the Author

B ill Howell has been an avid craft beer drinker and homebrewer since 1988. Upon retiring from the United States Navy in 2004, Bill moved to Alaska, where he blogs about the Alaskan craft brewing scene at Drinking on the Last Frontier (www.alaskanbeer.blogspot. com). In 2007, he created a beer appreciation course entitled "The Art and History of Brewing," which he teaches annually at the University of Alaska. In February 2010, Bill was selected as the Wynkoop Brewing Company's 2010 Beerdrinker of the Year at the annual competition in Denver, Colorado. He is the author of several books about craft beer in Alaska and serves as a media consultant to the Brewers Guild of Alaska.

Visit us at
www.historypress.net
....
This title is also available as an e-book